You Can Be Healed by Pastor Billy Joe will help take you into a new level of Faith. This book will bring you into an understanding—why the Lord wants you to walk and be totally whole; physically, emotionally, and spiritually. Not just for your sake, but so you can help others to press in and fulfill all that the Lord ordained and paid for when He made the ultimate sacrifice on the Cross of Calvary.

—Suzanne Hinn

YOU CAN
BE HEALED

YOU CAN BE HEALED

Billy Joe Daugherty

Destiny Image® Publishers, Inc.
P.O. Box 310
Shippensburg, PA 17257-0310

*"Speaking to the Purposes of God for This Generation
and for the Generations to Come"*

This book and all other Destiny Image, Revival Press, MercyPlace, Fresh Bread, Destiny Image Fiction, and Treasure House books are available at Christian bookstores and distributors worldwide.

Library of Congress Cataloging-in-Publication Data
Daugherty, Billy Joe.
You Can Be Healed / by Billy Joe Daugherty.
p. cm.
ISBN-13: 978-0-7684-2364-8 (pbk. : alk. paper)
-ISBN-10: 0-7684-2364-3

1. Spiritual healing—Biblical teaching.
2. Bible—Criticism, interpretation, etc. I. Title.

BS680.H4D38 2006
234'.131—dc22
2005033584

For a U.S. bookstore nearest you, call
1-800-722-6774.

For more information on foreign distributors, call
717-532-3040.

Or reach us on the Internet:
www.destinyimage.com

Printed in the U.S.A.

CONTENTS

INTRODUCTION

YOU can be healed by the power of God. God is no respecter of persons. What He has done for others, He will do for you! Jesus healed the sick 2,000 years ago, and the Bible says, "Jesus Christ is the same yesterday, today, and forever" (Heb. 13:8). God is just as willing to heal you as He is to heal anyone else.

As you read the words of this book, faith will come in your heart to be healed. "So then faith comes by hearing, and hearing by the word of God" (Rom. 10:17). In this book, you will read what the Word of God has to say about the healing of your body. God's Word is alive and full of power. It will drive out the darkness and sickness that tries to oppress your life.

You were not made to be sick. God originally planned for human beings to be well. Your body was designed to work in a state of health. Sickness is an invasion of an outlaw force seeking to rob you of your health. The knowledge of your covenant rights and privileges for being whole will enable you to stop the destruction of sickness, and the power of God will heal you.

Your inheritance of healing and wholeness is available now, in this life. *You can be healed now!*

Determine to get well. Decide that you are going to be healed. Decide to speak words of health rather than words of sickness. Begin to realize that you can do more for the Kingdom of God while you are living than when you are dead. The will to live and the will to get well are important issues in your healing because God works through faith. Faith is an exercise of your will to believe, confess, receive, and do what God says. Faith brings the expectation of the fulfillment of God's promises. Expect God to heal you!

Our heavenly Father wants His children to be well, just as any earthly father desires health for his children. God loves you. He cares about your life. He knows what you are going through. He wants to make you whole. In fact, this book has come to you as an expression of God's love for you.

You don't have to die before your time. You can live by the power of God. No matter what has been said about you, God's Word has the power to override the negative reports. Decide to believe God and let Him work miracles in your life! Refuse to die an untimely death from sickness or disease. You have the power in your will to say "no" to death and God will back you up with His power.

God has big plans for your life! " 'I know the thoughts that I think toward you,' says the Lord, 'thoughts of peace and not of evil, to give you a future and a hope' " (Jer. 29:11). That same verse in the New International Version says, " 'For I know the plans I have for you,' declares the Lord, 'plans to prosper you and not to harm you, plans to give you hope and a future.' "

The plans God has for you are good ones. There is a course He has ordained for you to run in this life. There are people who need what you have to give.

Remember, being whole involves more than just your own life. God's plan for you also calls for ministry to others.

There are people
who need what you
have to give.

Chapter 1

YOUR FAITH CAN MAKE YOU WHOLE

In Mark 5:25-34, we read the story of the woman who was plagued with an issue of blood for 12 years. She spent all the money she had to get well, yet she was no better. When she heard about Jesus, she began to say, "If only I may touch His clothes, I shall be made well." She went to Jesus and pressed through the crowd to touch Him. She had her heart set on touching Him, and nothing could stop her. When she got to Jesus, she touched Him, and immediately healing power flowed through her body. She was healed.

And Jesus, immediately knowing in Himself that power had gone out of Him, turned around in the crowd and said, "Who touched My clothes?" But His disciples said to Him, "You see the multitude thronging You, and You say, 'Who touched Me?'" And He looked around to see her who had done this thing. But the woman, fearing and trembling, knowing what had happened to her, came and fell down before Him and told Him the whole truth. And

He said to her, "Daughter, your faith has made you well. Go in peace, and be healed of your affliction."

Your faith can make you whole.

The words Jesus spoke to that woman are for all people of all times. Your faith can make you whole. Like this woman, you can touch Jesus today with your faith, and healing power can flow into you. God loves you as much as He loved this woman. She went after her healing and literally *drew* it out of Jesus. Faith will move you to pursue the things God has provided for your life.

It is valuable to study the story of this woman for two primary reasons. First, she was successful. As you study the actions of a person who successfully used her faith to be healed, you, too, can discover the principle for your own success. Second, you should study this woman's faith because Jesus commended her for her faith. Faith pleases God. Obviously, what this woman did pleased God.

Now, let's look at this passage more closely to discover how you can succeed with your faith, please God, and be healed.

Mark 5:25 reads, "Now a certain woman had a flow of blood for twelve years." Notice, it says, "a certain woman," not just a meaningless face in the crowd. You are a "certain" person, and God knows all about you. God knows your name, your circumstances, and where you are at this very moment.

Verse 26 says, "And [she] had suffered many things from many physicians. She had spent all that she had and was no better, but rather grew worse."

This woman knew a lot about suffering. Not only had she suffered from her sickness, but she had also suffered from the work of the doctors who were unable to help her. Disappointment filled her life. Twelve years of hurting and she was no better. At this point, hope must have all but left her.

You may be suffering terribly at this moment. The possibility of healing may seem far away. Perhaps you are now where this woman was. She received healing, and you can be healed, too. Get your head up; hope is not gone. Jesus is available, and you can get to Him.

Mark 5:27 says, "When she heard about Jesus, she came behind Him in the crowd and touched His garment."

Faith comes by hearing the Word of God (see Rom. 10:17). Maybe it was at the market, at the well, or at a neighbor's house where this woman heard about Jesus. When she heard about this man healing the sick and speaking the Scriptures with authority, something happened inside of her. She took the Word she heard and personally applied it to her own life.

Many people read the Bible and think of it as history or outstanding literature, but never interpret the message in relation to their own needs. Others hear testimonies of healing miracles and think of them as they do a fairy tale. They never relate that the miracles happening to others could happen to them.

This woman was different! When she heard of others being healed, she began to visualize her body being healed. If Jesus healed them, then she, too, could be healed. She took words she heard and treasured them as if God Himself had spoken them to her. The words moved her to action. She came to Jesus in spite of the crowds and obstacles. Since people were being healed by contact with Jesus, she wanted to touch Him, too.

Faith hears, speaks, believes, and then acts.

FAITH SPEAKS

This woman said, "If only I may touch His clothes, I shall be made well" (Mark 5:28). This woman spoke out what she believed in her heart. She spoke what she heard. She spoke what she was going to do. She spoke the results she expected.

The principle of faith is described in Second Corinthians 4:13: "And since we have the same spirit of faith, according to what is written, 'I believed and therefore I spoke,' we also believe and therefore speak."

The words you speak can express faith or doubt. The Word spoken in faith can lift you up from despair and discouragement, sickness and disease, into victory. Your words can open the door for a miracle to come your way.

> Faith hears, speaks, believes, and then acts.

"Death and life are in the power of the tongue" (Prov. 18:21). Words carry awesome power to destroy or to build, to give life or to kill. Jesus said, "For by your words you will be justified, and by your words you will be condemned" (Matt. 12:37). What you say about the healing power of God and your body will definitely have a bearing on your getting well.

When Jesus talked to people about having faith, He spoke to them not only about what they believed but also of what they spoke.

So Jesus answered and said to them, "Have faith in God. For assuredly, I say to you, whoever says to this mountain, 'Be removed and be cast into the sea,' and does not doubt in his heart, but believes that those things he says will be done, he will have whatever he says" (Mark 11:22-23).

Jesus said that faith is expressed by speaking what you believe, never doubting that it will come to pass. He said that you will have what you say when you believe what you say will come to pass. Faith begins with hearing God's Word, which you choose to believe as true for your own life. When you believe something in your heart, Jesus said it would come out of your mouth. Begin to speak what you believe of what you have heard from the Word of God.

The woman with the issue of blood spoke out what she had heard about Jesus healing the sick. She believed that the Word applied to her personally, and therefore, she dared to say, "I will be made whole." There was no doubt in her confession of faith, for the issue was settled in her heart.

The healing of the outer person begins with the vision of faith in the inner person. She saw it with the eye of faith and spoke of things that were not as though they already were (see Rom. 4:17). Healing happened in her heart and in her words before it happened in her body.

What the woman believed and spoke caused her to act. If you desire to do God's will, start with believing and speaking it. God told Joshua, "This Book of the Law shall not depart from your mouth, but you shall meditate in it day and night, that you may observe to do according to all that is written in it. For then you will make your way prosperous, and then you will have good success" (Josh. 1:8). Prosperity and success follow those who meditate, speak, and do the Word.

This same idea is again expressed in Proverbs 4:20-22:

My son, give attention to my words; incline your ear to my sayings. Do not let them depart from your eyes; keep them in the midst of your heart; for they are life to those who find them, and health to all their flesh.

Holding on to the Word of God and speaking it with your mouth in faith will bring health to your flesh. "He sent His word and healed them, and delivered them from their destructions" (Ps. 107:20). You can lay hold on the Word of God in the same way this woman laid hold on Jesus' garment. As you believe His Word in faith, healing virtue will flow into you.

YES, YOU HAVE FAITH

Jesus said, "Your faith has restored you to health...it has made you well...it has made you whole" (Mark 5:34). He is speaking this same word to you and me today. He is no respecter of persons. What He has done for one, He will do for another if the conditions are met.

You have faith today just as this woman had faith then. It was her faith in God that made her whole.

> Prosperity and success follow those who meditate, speak, and do the Word.

Romans 12:3 says, "God has dealt to each one a measure of faith." Your faith will increase as you hear the Word of God again and again and again.

The mountains you need to move are sickness, torment, affliction, and infirmity. Jesus said, "If you have faith as a mustard seed, you will say to this mountain, 'Move from here to there,' and it will move; and nothing will be impossible for you" (Matt. 17:20). Address the sickness in your body and tell it that it has to go. Command your blood, bones, cells, and organs to be healed and to function as God intended. Take authority and use the faith that Jesus has given you. He said your mountain would be removed if you doubt not in your heart. Hallelujah!

FAITH ACTS

Faith is active. It does something. The woman acted out her faith. She came to Jesus, boldly pressing through the massive crowd, and touched His garment.

In another passage, four friends tore open a roof to get a sick man to Jesus, demonstrating great faith. Let's look at this account from Mark 2:1-5,11-12:

*A*nd again He entered Capernaum after some days, and it was heard that He was in the house. Immediately many gathered together, so that there was no longer room to receive them, *not even near the door. And He preached the word to them. Then they came to Him, bringing a paralytic who was carried by four men. And when they could not come near Him because of the crowd, they uncovered the roof where He was. So when they had broken through, they let down the bed on which the paralytic was lying. When Jesus saw their faith, He said to the paralytic, "Son, your sins are forgiven you. ..."I say to you, arise, take up your bed, and go your way to your house." Immediately he arose, took up the bed, and went out in the presence of them all, so that all were amazed and glorified God, saying, "We never saw anything like this!"*

At a service we conducted in Omaha, Nebraska, a man came who had had a growth removed surgically from between his toes. During the surgery, some of the nerves and ligaments were severed, causing him to lose movement and feeling in his toes. After preaching the Word of faith on healing and praying for the people, I told them to do what they could not do before. As the man attempted to wiggle his toes, both feeling and movement returned to them. He came to the front and testified by taking his socks off and wiggling his toes in front of the entire congregation! He would not be denied! He refused to stay in the rut he was in! He rose up in faith and believed the Word of God.

There's no failure in God, so why should there be failure in you?

If there is something you can do to exercise your faith, do it! Faith acts. Even if nothing happens the first time, the first day, or the first week, don't give up. Never entertain thoughts of giving up. There's no failure in God, so why should there be failure in you? Be persistent! Keep striving to do what you could not do until the manifestation of your healing is obvious.

I'm sure you've had disappointments. The woman with the issue of blood was sick for 12 years and spent all her money to get well but instead got worse. She, too, must have battled the spirit of despair. She was possibly tempted to accept her sickness as her lot in life, but something happened when she heard of Jesus. She pressed through the hopeless feeling and wouldn't give up until she touched Jesus. You, too, can touch Jesus with your faith.

PARALYTICS ARE STILL BEING HEALED TODAY!

While we were preaching in Mexico in an outdoor stadium, a paralyzed man lay in the dust unable to walk by himself. Most of the people had never heard that Jesus loved them and wanted to heal their bodies. As I shared the Good News that Jesus came to bring abundant life, the man listened intently. Carried by friends to the meeting, the light of hope had almost gone out, but he heard that Jesus is alive and is healing the sick. He listened to the interpreter explain that we were going to pray and sickness would go from people as we commanded it to leave.

As we prayed, miracles began to happen. We called for those who had been healed to come forward and tell what

God had done. This paralyzed man got up, began walking, and stepped onto the elevated platform to share his story. We wept. On this dirty field, Jesus did exactly what He had done 2,000 years ago! He is alive, and you, too, can be healed!

You can break through the despair and hopelessness of a long illness. Reach up right now in faith believing and receive the resurrection power of Jesus Christ, which is available to make you completely whole.

Begin to thank Jesus for your healing today, even before it manifests. Faith believes before it receives!

HEALING PROMISES

Healing is yours because of the shed blood of Jesus Christ. The following promises are your legal inheritance from the Father God through the Lord Jesus Christ.

> To touch Jesus is to be made whole. I can touch Jesus today through prayer and faith (see Mark 5:25-34).

> The resurrection power of Jesus Christ flows from my tongue as I speak words of life (see Prov. 18:21).

> I have been given authority in the name of Jesus to speak to the mountains that I face. As I command the mountains of sickness, despair, hopelessness,

and lack to be removed in Jesus' name, they must go and be replaced with the fullness of God's blessings (see Mark 11:22-23).

Because I meditate on the Word of God day and night, God's prosperity and success are overtaking me in all realms of life (see Josh. 1:8).

I devour God's Word as a daily diet, for His Word is life and health to my flesh (see Prov. 4:20-22).

The measure of faith God gave me is growing by leaps and bounds (see Rom. 12:3).

Because my faith is growing, nothing is impossible unto me (see Matt. 17:20).

Faith believes
before it receives!

Chapter 2

HEALING IS GOD'S WILL FOR YOU

*B*eloved, I pray that you may prosper in all things and be in health, just as your soul prospers (3 John 2).

YOU can know Scriptures that promise healing, but if you don't know it is God's will to heal you, you will have a tough time receiving healing in your body. Perhaps the number one reason why people aren't healed today is they don't know healing belongs to them. They don't know it is God's will to heal them.

Hosea 4:6 says, "My people are destroyed for lack of knowledge." I want to help establish in you from the Word of God that healing is the will of God for your life. Healing is His will for you now—in this life.

I AM THE LORD WHO HEALS YOU

In Exodus 15, we read how God brought the children of Israel out of Egypt. He revealed Himself at the bitter waters of Marah. God showed Moses a branch to throw into the bitter waters—symbolic of the bitter waters of our life, which have been made sweet by the cross of Jesus Christ.

It was at the waters of Marah that God made a statute. He said, "If you will diligently heed the voice of the Lord your God and do what is right in His sight, give ear to His commandments and keep all His statutes, I will put none of the diseases on you which I have brought on the Egyptians. For I am the Lord who heals you" (Exod. 15:26).

The Egyptians had totally rejected God. They worshiped the creation instead of the Creator. Though God revealed Himself to them again and again, they still denied Him. They would not repent. Remember, the Egyptians were a type of the world or the enemy.

We need to realize that there's an opposite direction God takes His covenant people. He said to them (to the nation of Israel, and He's still speaking this to you and me today as believers), "I will take from you all sickness and all disease, *for I am the Lord your God who heals you.*"

Begin confessing Jesus not only as Savior and Lord, but as your Healer. It is God's nature to heal. In Hebrew, the name *Jehovah Rapha* or *Jehovah Rophe* is used to describe God as "Healer." He is the One who heals. *"I am the Lord who heals you."*

JESUS—TEACHING, PREACHING, HEALING

One of the three main thrusts of Jesus' ministry was healing. "And Jesus went about all Galilee, teaching in their synagogues, preaching the gospel of the kingdom, and healing all kinds of sickness and all kinds of disease among the people" (Matt. 4:23).

When someone gets healed, the Kingdom of God is revealed, for His Kingdom is a Kingdom of wholeness, of well-being, of life.

Jesus said, "I have come that they may have life, and that they may have it more abundantly" (John 10:10). The Amplified Version says it this way: "I came that they may have and enjoy life, and have it in abundance (to the full, till it overflows)."

When someone is healed, saved, delivered, mentally restored, or when a family is put back together, God's Kingdom is literally being established visibly in the earth.

Sickness and disease are works that come as a result of satan's entrance into the earth, which was not a part of God's original plan. Sickness and disease came as a result of Adam's rebellion. Sin, sickness, and disease entered the earth as a result of the thief who comes to steal, kill, and destroy. It is satan's plan to take health, vitality, and life away from people. "The thief [satan] does not come except to steal, and to kill, and to destroy" (John 10:10).

We can clearly see in Acts 10:38 that sickness is referred to as an oppression of the devil: "How God anointed Jesus of Nazareth with the Holy Spirit and with power, who went about doing good and healing all who were oppressed by the devil, for God was with Him."

Jesus' purpose was (and still is) to bring life, healing, and wholeness to mankind, to fulfill the statute made at the waters of Marah: *"I am the Lord who heals you!"* Jesus' purpose is to destroy the works of the devil (see 1 John 3:8).

I WILL TAKE SICKNESS AWAY FROM THE MIDST OF YOU

So you shall serve the Lord your God, and He will bless your bread and your water. And I will take sickness away from the midst of you (Exodus 23:25).

If you take sickness out of the midst of a person, what does he have? *Health! Healing! Wholeness!* Would you like sickness to be taken totally out of the midst of your family? Did you know this is a covenant promise?

You may say, "But that's in the Old Testament." True, but God hasn't changed as far as this promise is concerned. Jesus didn't do away with the Old Testament promises. In the New Testament, Jesus took sickness out of the midst of the people to show that God has never changed. God said, "I'll take sickness out of the midst of you."

When Jesus arrived on the scene, people wondered if He was the Messiah. In fact, when John the Baptist sent his followers to ask, "Are You the Coming One, or do we look for another?" (Matt. 11:3), Jesus gave only one answer:

*G*o and tell John the things which you hear
and see: The blind see and the lame walk;
the lepers are cleansed and the deaf hear; the dead
are raised up and the poor have the gospel
preached to them (Matthew 11:4-5).

Jesus came "doing" the Word. That's why we say, "God
has never changed. He's the same yesterday, today, and forever. He never alters His position. He was a healing God under
the Old Covenant; He is a healing God under the New
Covenant."

HEALING—
ONE OF GOD'S BENEFITS

*B*less the Lord, O my soul; and all that is within me, bless His holy name! Bless the Lord,
O my soul, and forget not all His benefits: Who
forgives all your iniquities, who heals all your diseases, who redeems your life from destruction,
who crowns you with lovingkindness and tender
mercies, who satisfies your mouth with good
things, so that your youth is renewed like the
eagle's (Psalm 103:1-5).

You are delivered from all your destructions. You are
crowned with lovingkindness and tender mercies. God will
renew your youth like the eagle's. That is, God will rekindle
your strength. He will rekindle your body. He will cause you

to mount up with wings as an eagle, because He sent His Word.

Healing is one of God's benefits. Healing is just as valid in this hour as forgiveness is valid in this hour. They're hooked together in verse 3. God forgives all your iniquities, and He also heals all your diseases. Hallelujah!

Forgiveness and healing are also hooked together in First Peter 2:24: "Who Himself [Jesus] bore our sins in His own body on the tree, that we, having died to sins, might live for righteousness—by whose stripes you were healed."

If you're saying God doesn't heal today, then you must also say He doesn't forgive sins today. Some people think healing came when Jesus arrived on earth. No! Healing has always been a part of God's nature.

> Healing has always been a part of God's nature.

HEALING—
AN OLD COVENANT PROVISION

Healing was a provision of the covenant with the children of Israel. Even though they rebelled against God and against Moses, a healing provision was made when they were bitten by serpents. As they looked upon the bronze serpent that Moses had prepared, they lived.

Then they journeyed from Mount Hor by the Way of the Red Sea, to go around the land of Edom; and the soul of the people became very discouraged on the way. And the people spoke against God and against Moses: "Why have you brought us up out of Egypt to die in the wilderness? For there is no food and no water, and our soul loathes this worthless bread." So the Lord sent fiery serpents among the people, and they bit the people; and many of the people of Israel died. Therefore the people came to Moses, and said, "We have sinned, for we have spoken against the Lord and against you; pray to the Lord that He take away the serpents from us." So Moses prayed for the people. Then the Lord said to Moses, "Make a fiery serpent, and set it on a pole; and it shall be that everyone who is bitten, when he looks at it, shall live." So Moses made a bronze serpent, and put it on a pole; and so it was, if a serpent had bitten anyone, when he looked at the bronze serpent, he lived (Numbers 21:4-9).

The serpent on the pole that Moses prepared is likened to Jesus in the New Covenant. Just as the pole with the fiery serpent was lifted up, even so must Jesus be lifted up to bring healing to us today. "And as Moses lifted up the serpent in the wilderness, even so must the Son of Man be lifted up" (John 3:14). He gives healing from sickness and forgiveness of sins under the New Covenant, which has better promises (see Heb. 8:6).

LIFT UP THE WORD OF HEALING

As we lift up Jesus (the living Word), just as the people were healed who looked upon Moses' brazen serpent under the Old Covenant, so today you can be forgiven and you can be healed. Through Jesus Christ, you can be delivered of mental torment, you can receive forgiveness of sins, you can be delivered of alcohol and drugs, you can be healed in your body, you can be made perfectly whole.

Psalm 107:20 says, "He sent His word and healed them, and delivered them from their destructions."

John 1:1 and 14 says: "In the beginning was the Word, and the Word was with God, and the Word was God. ...And the Word became flesh and dwelt among us, and we beheld His glory, the glory as of the only begotten of the Father, full of grace and truth." God's Word has been sent to you that you might be healed and delivered.

A man recently shared his testimony of how desperate he was because of some depressing situations he faced. He was tempted to end it all, and he was looking for a gun to kill himself. He said, "I heard a voice behind me speak, 'Matthew 4:4.' " It shocked him so much that he responded, "Huh?" He didn't even know what it meant, other than he recognized that it was a part of the Bible. He found a Bible and looked until he found Matthew 4:4, which reads, "Man shall not live by bread alone, but by every word that proceeds from the mouth of God." He came to Jesus, and his life was spared by the power of God's Word.

> God's Word has been sent to you that you might be healed and delivered.

You can step out and believe only that which you know. You must know God's promises for faith to come in your heart, so you can receive His healing power. Set your heart and mind on God's promises.

Become single-minded on God's Word. Don't be swayed by circumstances or you'll be robbed of God's healing power.

BE SINGLE-MINDED
ABOUT GETTING HEALED

Have you ever heard someone say, "Well, it could be that God made me sick for a reason"? Then, they turn right around and say, "I want God to heal me." That's a person of two minds. That is the person whom James calls "double-minded."

If you believe God put sickness on you, how can you pray to God to take it off of you? If God put it on you, then perhaps you need more sickness, maybe you need to get a double dose of it. If you're learning so much out of one dose of sickness, then just think how much more you could learn by three doses of it! (That's ridiculous when you think about it.)

How can you ask God to remove something that He gave to you? If He placed sickness upon you, then there must be a purpose for it. How could you contradict the will of God by asking for prayer if He put sickness on you? Does that make sense to you? The whole proposition of God making us sick is not only unscriptural but also illogical. When we understand what God has promised in His Word, we will begin to get a single mind. James says:

> *If any of you lacks wisdom, let him ask of God, who gives to all liberally and without reproach, and it will be given to him. But let him ask in faith, with no doubting, for he who doubts is like a wave of the sea driven and tossed by the wind. For let*

not that man suppose that he will receive anything from the Lord; he is a double-minded man, unstable in all his ways (James 1:5-8).

PUT YOUR EYES ON GOD'S WORD

Get your eyes off your circumstances and get them on the Word of God. The Word of God contains the power of God. The Word will save you from all works of darkness if you will believe it. Take the message of forgiveness of sin. If you mix faith with this message that you hear and it gets down into your heart, you say, "Lord, I believe that You forgive me," then the power of God is released to save you from sin. You believed and confessed in line with God's Word.

If you hear and believe the Good News that Jesus came to heal the brokenhearted and you are brokenhearted, you will acknowledge, "I receive healing of my broken heart. I receive healing of the grief, remorse, and sorrow that have come into my life." If you will believe it, the power of the gospel within you will work a healing from the brokenheartedness in your life.

Paul said, "For I am not ashamed of the gospel of Christ, for it is the power of God to salvation for everyone who believes, for the Jew first and also for the Greek" (Rom. 1:16).

The word *salvation* has multiple meanings. It means not only redemption from sin, but it also means healing, safety, preservation, wholeness, and soundness.

The Word of God is the power of God in you, as a born-again believer, unto your healing, unto your safety and preservation, unto your wholeness and soundness.

> Don't be swayed by circumstances or you'll be robbed of God's healing power.

My son, give attention to my words; incline your ear to my sayings. Do not let them depart from your eyes; keep them in the midst of your heart; for they are life to those who find them, and health to all their flesh (Proverbs 4:20-22).

Like the writer of the above verses, God says, "Give attention to My words." If you are going to purchase a new house, you will give attention to the newspaper ads about houses for sale or you will spend hours talking to a realtor. You might even spend hours driving around, looking at new houses. Or you may pick up a multi-list book. Perhaps you'll pick up a magazine that advertises houses, apartments, condos, townhouses, or whatever you need. You will literally give hours, weeks, or perhaps months searching for "just the right house" for you.

You need to be as diligent in seeking your healing. After all, **how badly do you need to be healed?** *How important is healing to you?* How important is it for you and your family to stay well and not die an untimely death from sickness or disease?

The attention you give to the word of healing is determined by how much you value health in your life and how you value the Word of God.

Some folks have said, "This healing stuff just doesn't work." If a farmer's seed is tossed out and lands on a carpet or on concrete, there is no reason to expect that seed to produce a harvest. In a similar way, many people have heard about healing. They have heard a preacher speak about it, but it's like seed lying on the top of the ground. You must get that seed in the center of your heart and keep it there if you expect to reap a crop of healing. No farmer takes the seed out of the ground and says, "I'm going to keep it in there a few hours and then I'm going to pull it out." A farmer who wants the harvest leaves the seed in the ground.

We're focusing on physical healing, but these same principles apply to all areas of wholeness—spirit, soul, body, family, and finances. Healing is for the whole man.

HEALING PROMISES

God wants you to be well. Speak these promises aloud and meditate daily upon them.

By Jesus' stripes I am healed (see 1 Pet. 2:24).

It is God's will that I prosper and be in health, just as my soul prospers (see 3 John 2).

God says, "I am the Lord who heals you" (Exod. 15:26); "I came that you may enjoy life and have it in overflowing abundance" (John 10:10); "I will take sickness from the midst of you" (Exod. 23:25).

Healing is one of God's benefits for me (see Ps. 103:3).

Jesus is the serpent on the pole lifted up in the new covenant for my healing and deliverance (see John 3:14).

God sent His Word and healed me (see Ps. 107:20).

I pay attention to God's Word, for it is life and health to me (see Prov. 4:20-22).

God's Word
is the platform
from which
faith is launched.

Chapter 3

SCRIPTURAL EVIDENCE FOR YOUR HEALING

Y OUR faith for healing cannot go beyond your knowledge of the Word, for God's Word is the platform from which faith is launched.

Faith is something you no longer doubt. It is something you know. You are so confident of knowing it that you believe to the point that you will speak it, and you will do it. Faith is hearing, believing, speaking, and doing God's Word. Romans 10:17 says, "So then faith comes by hearing, and hearing by the word of God."

Meditation on God's Word is one key to developing your faith, while praise and action are keys to releasing it. When we know what God says about healing, then we have a basis to believe God. Probably the number one reason why most people are not healed today is lack of knowledge. They simply don't know that God wants to heal them. They may know that God has healed someone else. They may know a Bible verse or two where Jesus healed someone in the Scriptures, but that is just history to them. The issue is to know that healing belongs to you today. Until you know from the Word of God that healing belongs to you, you won't grab hold and take it as yours. You must know that you know that you know that healing is yours down in your own *"knower"*!

In the beginning when God made Adam and Eve, there was no sickness in the Garden. There was no disease. The presence of the devil was not yet made known. Everything God made was good. "Then God saw everything that He had made, and indeed it was very good" (Gen. 1:31).

God gave Adam the right to rule the world, but Adam sold his lease to the devil through disobedience.

When the new Heaven and the new earth come, there will be no sickness. Because of Jesus' victory over sin, sickness, and poverty at Calvary, we have been given the authority now in this earth to resist the works of satan and be victorious over them. As we take our stance on the Word of God, unwavering, holding fast to God's promises, sickness and disease can be removed from your body.

Let's get a glimpse of what the New Jerusalem will be like.

*N*ow *I saw a new heaven and a new earth, for the first heaven and the first earth had passed away. Also there was no more sea. Then I, John, saw the holy city, New Jerusalem, coming down out of heaven from God, prepared as a bride adorned for her husband. And I heard a*

loud voice from heaven saying, "Behold, the tab-
ernacle of God is with men, and He will dwell
with them, and they shall be His people. God
Himself will be with them and be their God. And
God will wipe away every tear from their eyes;
there shall be no more death, nor sorrow, nor
crying. There shall be no more pain, for the for-
mer things have passed away." Then He who sat
on the throne said, "Behold, I make all things
new." And He said to me, "Write, for these
words are true and faithful." And He said to me,
"It is done! I am the Alpha and the Omega, the
Beginning and the End. I will give of the foun-
tain of the water of life freely to him who thirsts.
He who overcomes shall inherit all things, and I
will be his God and he shall be My son"
(Revelation 21:1-7).

If there was no sickness in the beginning, and there's
going to be no sickness in the end, why would God want sickness in the middle? It surely must be God's will that man live
without sickness now. Somewhere in God's plan He didn't
just say, "Well, let's throw sickness on them until this whole
thing is over in order that We can help develop them." No! We
find out from Genesis 3 that as satan stepped on the scene, not
only did war, strife, murder, and all the other works of the
flesh enter, not only did the curse pass upon the whole earth,
but physical sickness also began to affect and oppress
mankind.

There is a time to die. "To everything there is a season, a
time for every purpose under heaven: a time to be born, and

a time to die" (Eccles. 3:1-2). However, Scripture does not say, "It's appointed for man to die an excruciating, terrifying, tormenting death by cancer." That's not in the Bible. The Bible does not say, "It's appointed unto man once to die on the freeway." Nowhere in Scripture will you find that kind of thinking. Men will die if Jesus does not come. Great Christians have been martyred for their testimony of Jesus, but that is not the same as sickness and disease. How then are we to die? The Scripture says, "You take away their breath, they die and return to their dust" (Ps. 104:29). When you have finished your course and kept the faith, there is a way to die in God's time.

GOD WANTS YOU TO BE WELL

Third John 2 says, "Beloved, I pray that you may prosper in all things and be in health, just as your soul prospers." John was expressing the very heart of God for your life. "I wish, I pray, I desire more than you can ever imagine, that you prosper, that you be blessed in your family, blessed in your mind, blessed in your life. I want everything you touch to prosper, and I want you to be in health. I want you to be strong. I made man for wholeness, not for sickness nor for the mental ward. I made man to stand upright and rule and reign in the earth." Hallelujah! You were made to rule and reign! Sickness, disease, sin, and poverty are not to have the rule over you.

Why has the devil struck with sickness and disease? Because man was made for the glory and honor of God. We were made to reflect the very likeness and presence of the Lord. When you are blessing God and doing what He has called you to do, you are fulfilling your divine purpose in life and God's glory radiates from you. When the devil strikes you, he strikes at God's glory.

Perhaps your calling is to be a mother to your children. Satan has removed more than one mother from this divine calling prematurely, but you and I as believers have the power to stop satan's works. However, we must first come into agreement that it is God's will to heal.

DOES YOUR CHURCH TEACH HEALING?

Jesus said, "Take heed what you hear" (Mark 4:24). A noted teacher and evangelist talks about the importance of what you hear, the importance of attending a church that teaches the full truth of the Word of God. He shares, "My mother grew up in a church where they taught that healing was not for today. They taught that it was God's will for some to be sick. As a result, she died at the age of 37 and left me as a little boy with no mother. This was all because she went to the wrong church. She could have lived if she had known what the Word of God has to say about healing and then put her agreement with it." This evangelist has seen many people healed of the very same disease that killed his mother. *What you hear and where you go to church are important!*

If you give great attention to hearing the Word of healing, it will come back to you. The message of healing will give back to you in the same way that you give to it. If there's nothing given to hearing the Word, then there will be nothing to come back to you in fulfillment when the crisis hour hits and you are in need. It's hard to get water out of a well that hasn't been dug! Have you dug the well to draw the water of healing out of the well of salvation? Isaiah 12:3 says, "Therefore with joy you will draw water from the wells of salvation." Have you dug deep into the Word on healing?

There is an immune system in our faith. You build up an immunization against a particular disease when it tries to come and touch your body. You may be exposed to something, but it has no effect on you when you have the proper immunity. God's Word is "medicine" that provides the immunity against sickness and disease, poverty and lack, or any other work of the devil.

The work of the enemy is not difficult to identify. As James 1:17 says, "Every good gift and every perfect gift is from above, and comes down from the Father of lights, with whom there is no variation or shadow of turning." God sends only good and perfect gifts. Obviously, sickness and disease are not good and perfect gifts! They come from the author of sickness, disease, and every evil work—satan himself.

> God's Word is "medicine" that provides the immunity against sickness and disease, poverty and lack, or any other work of the devil.
>
>

WHAT ABOUT MEDICINE?

I'm not against medicine, doctors, or nurses, for they are fighting the same enemy we are. I'm for what gets people well and in relationship with Jesus. I believe the wisdom a doctor has about getting people well comes from God, because the devil doesn't go around giving doctors information on how to get people well when he is the one who made them sick.

Medicine doesn't fall out of space from the devil. It comes out of God's earth. God put all the elements into the earth, and He gave someone the wisdom and knowledge to extract those things out of the earth and use them. If you are taking medicine, just say, "Thank You, Father, You are the Creator of heaven and earth. This is part of Your earth. It has been put together in wisdom and it will minister healing. I take this medicine by faith."

Don't get flaky or weird or go off the deep end and come against doctors and medicine. The uniting of medicine and prayer can be a powerful force against sickness and disease. As an example, if you need a shot against yellow fever or typhus and tablets for malaria before going into a foreign country, take them. Add your prayer to it that God will protect you.

You can inoculate yourself with the Word of God to build up an immunization in your body to sickness and disease. If your spirit is infused with the Word of God, when sickness or disease try to attack your body, you can quickly say, "No way!"

In the name of Jesus, you can refuse sickness and disease. James said, "Therefore submit to God. Resist the devil and he will flee from you" (James 4:7).

Sickness and disease are of the devil (see Acts 10:38). If you are first submitted to God as a believer, then you can resist the devil in the name of Jesus and he and his goods have no choice but to flee (see James 4:6-8).

GOD'S WILLINGNESS TO HEAL

Most people believe God is able to heal because He can do anything. The issue is not the ability of God. The issue is, "Does God want to heal me? Is He willing to heal me?"

When someone is attacked with sickness or disease and says, "It must have been the Lord's will," or "I've accepted this as the Lord's will," they are not deliberately accusing God of causing the sickness, yet such statements are the same as accusing God.

We must understand the power of our words when we say, "It must be the Lord's will" when sickness and disease come.

The leper came to Jesus and said, "If You are willing, You can make me clean." In other words, "I know You are able, but do You want to heal me?"

When He [Jesus] had come down from the mountain, great multitudes followed Him. And behold, a leper came and worshiped Him, saying, "Lord, if You are willing, You can make me clean." Then Jesus put out His hand and touched him, saying, "I am willing; be cleansed." And immediately his leprosy was cleansed (Matthew 8:1-3).

The whole world is asking, "Lord, are You willing to heal me? Do You really love me? Do You want to help me? Do You want to heal me?"

Empty religion has said, "God is concerned about more important things than your healing." But Jesus settled the issue once and for all when He told the leper, "I am willing to heal you...be cleansed."

THIRTY-EIGHT YEARS SICK—
HEALED BY JESUS

The man at the pool of Bethesda wasn't certain of God's willingness to heal him. Let's look at this account from John 5:2-9.

*N*ow *there is in Jerusalem by the Sheep Gate a pool, which is called in Hebrew, Bethesda, having five porches. In these lay a great multitude of sick people, blind, lame, paralyzed, waiting for the moving of the water. For an angel went down at a certain time into the pool and stirred up the water; then whoever stepped in first, after the stirring of the water, was made well of whatever disease he had. Now a certain man was there who had an infirmity thirty-eight years. When Jesus saw him lying there, and knew that he already had been in that condition a long time, He said to him, "Do you want to be made well?" The sick man answered Him, "Sir, I have no man to put me into the pool when the water is stirred up, but while I am coming, another steps down before me." Jesus said unto him, "Rise, take up your bed and walk." And immediately the man was made well, took up his bed, and walked. And that day was the Sabbath.*

Thirty-eight years is a long time to be sick and unable to get up. It appears this man had almost resigned himself to never being healed. The pool was a place where some had been healed; however, this man told Jesus he had no one to help him into the water when it was troubled. He was close to a miracle, but he had never received one.

Jesus spoke to this man, "Do you want to be made well?" He was touching the key issue for his miracle—*his will*. Do you will to be made whole? Is your will committed to getting well? The will of an individual is the catalyst for faith to be released. *Through your will, you choose to have what God wills for you.* Your will can decide to believe or doubt. The choice is yours. Therefore, Jesus talked to the man about his will.

Some people who should have died from so-called incurable diseases have lived. Others have died when they should have lived. There is a strong belief among most doctors that the will to live is a major factor in the healing process.

DETERMINED TO LIVE!

We have a lady, named Julie, in our congregation who had a chronic lung problem since the age of 16, suffered many hospitalizations and treatments, and in 1969 entered the hospital with her lungs totally collapsed. After being examined by several physicians, she was told that she would not live two months, to accept it and prepare for death.

But Julie knew that God's will for her was only for good. She did not accept the bad news. Just as Joshua and Caleb did not accept an evil report, she refused to entertain predictions that were contrary to God's Word. Her doctors shook their

> *Through your will, you choose to have what God wills for you.*

heads as she insisted that she was not going to die!

Julie had several opportunities to become discouraged. She was hospitalized two or three more times in the course of the next eight years. But in 1977, as she was sitting high in the balcony at a seminar on the ORU campus, Brother Roberts looked straight up at her section and said, "Something's going on in the balcony!"

It was the day of Julie's miracle! God spoke to her heart and told her she was healed! For years she had not taken a breath without wheezing. God told her to try out her healing by running around the ORU track and that she would neither wheeze nor tire. She obeyed. On the ORU indoor track, she took off running while one of the students stood by counting the laps. At the end of laps that totalled eight and a half miles, God finally said, "What does it take to convince you that you're healed?" So she told the student that she'd better stop before God got mad at her!

Julie has been running and walking ever since. In fact, she does not even own a car. She walks to church, walks to buy groceries, and is in better health than she has ever been in her life! She made up her mind that she was going to live and not die!

Your will is just as important today. Set your will to be healed. Determine to believe and desire to be whole. Remove the doubt and wavering attitude.

Begin to thank Jesus for His willingness to heal you. Say it aloud: "I thank You, Jesus, for healing me."

THE SPOKEN WORD BROUGHT HEALING

Jesus healed the centurion's servant through the spoken word. People can be healed through the spoken Word of God today, for Jesus has never changed.

Now when Jesus had entered Capernaum, a centurion came to Him, pleading with Him, saying, "Lord, my servant is lying at home paralyzed, dreadfully tormented." And Jesus said to him, "I will come and heal him." The centurion answered and said, "Lord, I am not worthy that You should come under my roof. **But only speak a word, and my servant will be healed.** *For I also am a man under authority, having soldiers under me. And I say to this one, 'Go,' and he goes; and to another, 'Come,' and he comes; and to my servant, 'Do this,' and he does it." When Jesus heard it, He marveled, and said to those who followed, "Assuredly, I say to you, I have not found such great faith, not even in Israel! And I say to you that many will come from east and west, and sit down with Abraham, Isaac, and Jacob in the kingdom of heaven. But the sons of the kingdom will be cast out into outer darkness. There will be weeping and gnashing of teeth"* (Matthew 8:5-12).

Here was a Roman centurion who had greater faith than those who were of Abraham, and Jesus makes a comparison. He acknowledged that the centurion came on the basis of faith.

*T*hen Jesus said to the centurion, "Go your way; and as you have believed, so let it be done for you." And his servant was healed that same hour (Matthew 8:13).

HEALED FROM DEPRESSION

One of our care pastors tells of having lived for many years in multiplied depression, overcome with fear, not wanting to be around people other than her immediate family. She had withdrawn further and further into a shell of isolation, to the point that she could not even leave the house and was constantly tormented with fear of having to go to a mental hospital.

But Shirley Morton attended an Easter morning service in 1981 that changed her life! As the Word of God was preached, and the entire service seemed to be prepared especially for her, a new life began to rise up within her. Joy and peace flooded the once tormented soul. Shirley was delivered by the power of God's Word!

In her own words, now ten years later, Shirley testifies, "The gentle message of Jesus' love and healing had done its work. The search was over. The hope had been returned and faith did its perfect work. I had allowed the message of God's faithfulness—no matter how it looks in the natural or how long you have waited—to be real to me again. The Word prevailed and a perfect miracle of restoration was done. This was just like being brought back from the dead, because that is exactly what it was like in the condition I was in. It occurred in the year that I was 50—my year of Jubilee! Life is full and good and His mercy and grace continue to bless by life!"

Glory to God! The simple gospel message brings deliverance and restoration!

Jesus cast out devils with a word.

When evening had come, they brought to Him many who were demon-possessed. And He cast out the spirits with a word, and healed all who were sick, that it might be fulfilled which was spoken by Isaiah the prophet, saying, "He Himself took our infirmities and bore our sicknesses" (Matthew 8:16-17).

A TOUCH BROUGHT HEALING

Jesus also healed with a touch. A touch from a believer who is filled with the power of the Holy Spirit will bring healing to the sick today.

Now when Jesus had come into Peter's house, He saw his wife's mother lying sick with a fever. And He touched her hand, and the fever left her. Then she arose and served them (Matthew 8:14-15).

Basically, there are three ways Jesus healed: through the spoken Word, with a touch, or through a combination of the spoken Word and a touch.

You can be touched today by Jesus through another human being. Jesus said He would come and indwell believers. He gave authority to believers saying, "They will lay hands on the sick, and they will recover" (Mark 16:18).

HEALED THROUGH LAYING ON OF HANDS

Joseph Jabbour is a restaurant owner in Tulsa. In 1988 he was invited to a Food Show in Nevada. While there, during some free time he decided to try out the go-cart track at an amusement area.

While sitting in his go-cart, Joseph was suddenly struck from behind by one of the cars, which was going at full speed. The impact was so severe that he suffered a break in his left ankle, right knee, right thumb, and a ruptured disk in his back.

In time the breaks healed, but there was no relief for the ruptured disk. Examinations and X-rays were repeated over and over both in Nevada and Oklahoma during the next year. All the while, Joseph was in excruciating pain. He could not get in or out of the car without help; nor could he bend over to pick up a menu dropped on the floor. If he turned his body, he would experience paralysis. The ruptured disk could be felt protruding beneath the skin of his back.

Many times he had been told by orthopedic specialists that without surgery there would be no relief from pain and the paralysis would become permanent. Joseph refused.

Joseph's miracle came in 1989, on the busiest night of the week for someone in the restaurant business: a Saturday! As he was trying to keep pace and host the flood of customers, Joseph was in severe pain. Just moving at all was a challenge.

When Sharon and I walked in, Joseph greeted us hurriedly and then walked on to tend to others. However, as he was proceeding away from us, he later told us that an inner voice said distinctly to him to "turn around and have Billy Joe pray for your back."

When Joseph returned to our table, I reached out my hand and touched his back, prayed a simple prayer of faith and he left.

Within five minutes, as he later testified, there was absolutely no pain in Joseph's back! He could turn. He could bend. He could no longer feel the protruding disk. X-rays have followed that showed every disk being totally normal, as if nothing had ever happened! In the two-year period until the present, Joseph has had no back problems whatsoever and has witnessed to many people of the night that God healed him!

When a believer touches, Jesus is touching. We're not touching in our name, but in His name. We're not touching just by our spirit. We're touching with His Spirit. We're not touching at our own word, but we're touching in His Word. So, it is Jesus' life flowing through us that is touching others when we lay hands on them for their healing.

Since God's Word has not lost any of its power, when the Word of God is spoken and you receive it as such, you will receive His healing power!

JESUS' MINISTRY THRUST— TEACHING, PREACHING, HEALING

Jesus' entire ministry was devoted to teaching, preaching, and healing.

*T*hen Jesus went about all the cities and vil-
lages, teaching in their synagogues, preaching the gospel of the kingdom, and healing every
sickness and every disease among the people
(Matthew 9:35).

If Jesus went about teaching, preaching, and healing 2,000 years ago, and Hebrews 13:8 says He is the same yesterday, today, and forever, what is God's will for you today? How many people did Jesus make sick in the New Testament? Obviously, none!

Then, if there are occasions where God makes people sick for His glory, why can't we find cases in the New Testament where Jesus told people, "I'm sorry, but you must stay sick for the glory of God"? The only time Jesus ever mentioned anything close to that was concerning a blind man getting healed, and the glory was not in the man being blind. The glory was in the blindness being removed (see John 9:1-7). That's how the Father was glorified.

Some people have said, "I'm going to glorify God through my sickness." However, the Word of God indicates that you will glorify God through your healing. It's when the sick are healed that people begin to magnify and glorify God. Of course, if you are sick, it is right to praise and glorify God for who He is, but not for your sickness. Yes, glorify God in your time of sickness by being a witness and showing His love. Seek the Lord, live His life, and declare His goodness, but don't resign yourself that sickness is God's will for you.

In the case of a loss of limbs, there is obviously a need for a creative miracle. This is something different from divine healing. It comes under the working of miracles in First Corinthians 12:4-8. It happens as the Spirit wills, but it is not totally independent of our faith. In other words, don't give up on a miracle but, at the same time, believe God for the grace to do His will right now. There are quadriplegics who have not allowed physical handicaps to stop them from being all God wants them to be. They are doing His will.

If you can settle the issue in your heart that it is the will of God to heal you, healing can come to you. God wants to heal you. God is willing to heal you.

Because you have made the Lord, who is my refuge, even the Most High, your dwelling place, no evil shall befall you, nor shall any plague come near your dwelling; for He shall give His angels charge over you, to keep you in all your ways (Psalm 91:9-11).

If no plague comes near your dwelling place, what does that leave you with? Health!

Jesus said that we should pray to the Father, "Your kingdom come. Your will be done on earth as it is in heaven" (Matt. 6:10).

How much sickness and disease are in Heaven? How much health is up there? There's no sickness and disease in Heaven!

Not one drop! So, we're to pray the manifestation of God's healing power into the earth.

HEALING PROMISES

God wants you to be well, and He is both able and willing to heal you today. Meditate upon the following promises and speak them aloud daily.

God wants me to prosper and be in health, just as my soul prospers (see 3 John 2).

God gives me only good and perfect gifts. He has no sickness or disease to give me (see James 1:17).

As I submit to God and resist the devil, he must flee from me. Sickness and disease must flee from me (see James 4:7).

Jesus is able and willing to heal me (see Matt. 8:1-2).

Jesus can heal me through my believing, receiving, and speaking His Word or through the touch of another believer who is empowered by the Holy Spirit (see Mark 16:18).

Jesus already paid for all sin and sickness at Calvary (see Matt. 8:17).

Jesus is the same yesterday, today, and forever (see Heb. 13:8).

Because the Lord is my refuge and habitation, no evil or plague shall come nigh my dwelling (see Ps. 91:9-11).

NO CONDEMNATION

The message of this book is: *You Can Be Healed.* Nothing is written to judge, condemn, or belittle anyone who is sick. I have fought sickness at times and so has my family. What has helped us the most are the powerful words of faith written about in this book. Pity may give comfort to your emotions, but it won't get you healed. Compassion, on the other hand, is God's love that dares to speak the truth boldly. This book is God's love coming to you to get you well. Don't allow one thought of condemnation to enter your mind. God is for you and so am I.

Chapter 4

REDEEMED FROM THE CURSE

You were not redeemed with corruptible things, like silver or gold, from your aimless conduct received by tradition from your fathers, but with the precious blood of Christ, as of a lamb without blemish and without spot (1 Peter 1:18-19).

THE blood of Jesus Christ was shed that we might be delivered from the hands of the enemy.

If you ever wonder how valuable you are, just remember the price that was paid for you—Jesus' blood. When you look in the mirror, you ought to say, "I am valuable property." Now, that's not exalting you. That is exalting the blood that was paid for you. It is realizing the worth God places on your life.

Redemption means God never quits believing in the man He has created. He never quits believing man can walk, talk, fellowship with Him, and be in the place of dominion that He ordained for him to be.

God saw Himself in us. Though a fractured, broken image of what He originally intended, He saw that He could put us back together again through His redemption plan. Paul talks about our redemption from the curse in Galatians.

O foolish Galatians! Who has bewitched you that you should not obey the truth, before whose eyes Jesus Christ was clearly portrayed among you as crucified? This only I want to learn from you: Did you receive the Spirit by the works of the law, or by the hearing of faith? Are you so foolish? Having begun in the Spirit, are you now being made perfect by the flesh? (Galatians 3:1-3).

Paul talks about faith and the Spirit, and then he talks about the law and the flesh. He draws a comparison on where the Galatians are, having moved out of faith and out of the Spirit into the flesh and into the works of the law.

Have you suffered so many things in vain—if indeed it was in vain? Therefore He who supplies the Spirit to you and works miracles among you, does He do it by the works of the law, or by the hearing of faith?—just as Abraham "believed God, and it was accounted to him for righteousness" (Galatians 3:4-6).

ABRAHAM GOT IT BY FAITH

Abraham became righteous by faith. He believed God.

Therefore know that only those who are of faith are sons of Abraham. And the Scripture, foreseeing that God would justify the Gentiles by faith, preached the gospel to Abraham beforehand, saying, "In you all the nations shall be blessed." So then those who are of faith are blessed with believing Abraham (Galatians 3:7-9).

God foresaw that you and I were going to be justified by faith, not by the works of the law or the deeds of the flesh. Therefore, He preached the gospel to Abraham and said, "In you all the nations of the earth will be blessed." He was preaching about Jesus, because Jesus was the seed of Abraham. The seed was in the loins of Abraham even at that time when he believed in faith. Abraham conceived faith inside of him, and ultimately, it was through Abraham's descendants that Jesus came into the earth.

Today, those who believe the gospel have the same faith as Abraham had. Abraham believed the gospel, and we believe the gospel. He walked by faith, and we are to walk by faith. He had to listen to the Spirit of God, and we have to listen to the Spirit of God. He set a pattern for us to follow.

*F*or as many as are of the works of the law are under the curse; for it is written, "Cursed is everyone who does not continue in all things which are written in the book of the law, to do them" (Galatians 3:10).

Here's the definition of the curse: For as many as are under the works of the law are under the curse. Paul is saying, "If you are under the works of the law, then you are in the flesh, and in that position, you are under the curse." Why would you be under a curse if you were living under the law? Primarily because you can't keep the works of the law. We are incapable of keeping all of the laws of God. If we don't have God's grace and mercy, we have no hope. If we don't have the blood of Christ, we are doomed.

Here we find the curse of man is breaking the law of God. This curse goes all the way back to Genesis. It's not just the curse of breaking the Mosaic law. It's the curse of breaking the law of God laid down to Adam and Eve when He said:

*O*f every tree of the garden you may freely eat; but of the tree of the knowledge of good and evil you shall not eat, for in the day that you eat of it you shall surely die (Genesis 2:16-17).

They violated the law of God and the curse came upon them. God had a law from the very beginning, yet we have the amplification of it in Moses.

*B*ut that no one is justified by the law in the sight of God is evident, for "The just shall live by faith" (Galatians 3:11).

That is, the righteous person will obtain his life by faith. The just shall live by faith. You can't be in right standing with God by keeping the works of the law. It's a work of God's grace and mercy, which you receive through exercising faith in God and in His Word, that provides righteousness.

*Y*et the law is not of faith, but "the man who does them shall live by them" (Galatians 3:12).

When the curse came, it affected every part of man's existence. We see in Adam that his children fought against one another, sickness and disease entered the world, and a curse came on everything that was a part of man. That curse is amplified in Deuteronomy 28. All of these things have been happening since Adam.

Paul says in Galatians 3:13-14:

*C*hrist has redeemed us from the curse of the law, having become a curse for us, (for it is written, "Cursed is everyone who hangs on a tree"), that the blessing of Abraham might come upon the Gentiles in Christ Jesus, that we might receive the promise of the Spirit through faith.

Now, what is the curse? If you have ever read the curses in Deuteronomy 28, you will thank the Lord that you are redeemed from them.

CURSES OF DISOBEDIENCE

God's will for man has always been blessing. God's will for man is provision and abundance. But He said, "If you transgress My law, these curses will come upon you." Does that mean God wants these curses to come on people? Of course not! However, they did come out of the spoken Word of God. In other words, God said these are going to come if disobedience reigns. It was not His will, but He is a holy God, and He spoke the consequences of sin.

When a person violates the law of God, he moves out of the blessings of God into the realm where he will be attacked by the devil...where certain laws, instead of working for man, will work against him.

For example, electricity can work for you, but if you misuse it, it can work against your body to the point of death! The electricity ultimately came from God, but if someone is electrocuted, do we blame God? No! A law was violated causing the person to be electrocuted.

It is not the will of God that any person experience the curse. Yet, if a law is violated, a door is open for the curse to come. Let's review these curses of Deuteronomy 28, and for every verse you read, give thanks to God that you are redeemed from it!

*B*ut *it shall come to pass, if you do not obey the voice of the Lord your God, to observe*

God doesn't want us to be cursed. But when we misuse the law, that happens.

carefully all His commandments and His statutes which I command you today, that all these curses will come upon you and overtake you: Cursed shall you be in the city, and cursed shall you be in the country. Cursed shall be your basket and your kneading bowl. Cursed shall be the fruit of your body and the produce of your land, the increase of your cattle and the offspring of your flocks. Cursed shall you be when you come in, and cursed shall you be when you go out (Deuteronomy 28:15-19).

Take time to read Deuteronomy 28:15-68 and see how the curse affected every part of a person's existence.

Thank God we're redeemed from the curse! Much of the world is under the curse right now. That's why there are so many mental institutions, hospitals, drug addicts and alcoholics, and so much divorce. All of the evil you are seeing on the earth is a result of the curse. The Good News is: We've been redeemed from it! Every person who will put his faith and trust in Jesus Christ can be redeemed from the curse!

When Jesus hung on the tree at Calvary, God allowed the curse to fall on Him. Jesus was made a curse for us. He took the curse in your place.

When you study your redemption from the curse, you will love Jesus more than you have ever loved Him before. You will realize what Gethsemane was all about. Jesus took upon Himself the curse of the whole world. The Bible says His physical appearance was so marred at the crucifixion that He didn't even have the appearance of a man (see Isa. 52:14). He took upon Himself all sickness and all disease. He was made a curse for us. He literally took every curse listed in Deuteronomy 28 as He hung on that cross in order for you to receive all the blessings of Abraham.

BLESSINGS OF OBEDIENCE

Deuteronomy 28:1-14 gives us an amplification of these blessings. Let's take a look at the good side of this deal!

Now it shall come to pass, if you diligently obey the voice of the Lord your God, to observe carefully all His commandments which I command you today, that the Lord your God will set you high above all nations of the earth. And all these blessings shall come upon you and overtake you, because you obey the voice of the Lord your God: Blessed shall you be in the city, and blessed shall you be in the country. Blessed shall be the fruit of your body, the produce of your ground and the increase of your herds, the increase of your cattle and the offspring of your flocks. Blessed shall be your basket and your kneading bowl. Blessed shall you be when you come in, and blessed shall you be when you go out. The Lord will cause your enemies who rise against you to be defeated before your face; they shall come out against you one way and flee before you seven ways. The Lord will command the blessing on you in your storehouses and in all

> Our God reigns in all realms!

to which you set your hand, and He will bless you in the land which the Lord your God is giving you. The Lord will establish you as a holy people to Himself, just as He has sworn to you, if you keep the commandments of the Lord your God and walk in His ways. Then all peoples of the earth shall see that you are called by the name of the Lord, and they shall be afraid of you. And the Lord will grant you plenty of goods, in the fruit of your body, in the increase of your livestock, and in the produce of your ground, in the land of which the Lord swore to your fathers to give you. The Lord will open to you His good treasure, the heavens, to give the rain to your land in his season, and to bless all the work of your hand. You shall lend to many nations, but you shall not borrow. And the Lord will make you the head and not the tail; you shall be above only, and not be beneath, if you heed the commandments of the Lord your God, which I command you today, and are careful to observe them. So you shall not turn aside from any of the words which I command you this day, to the right hand or to the left, to go after other gods to serve them.

Hallelujah for God's blessings! The blessings of Abraham will come on you as you put your faith in Jesus Christ. One of the blessings is that you will have the presence of the Holy Spirit in your life. God will dwell inside of you. Jesus, the seed, will be in you. You will be blessed in your body. Instead of the curse of sickness and disease, you will walk in health. Instead of the curse on your family, God will keep your family. It's not right for your children to serve the devil.

All of us have been affected by the curse in one way or another, and all of us can be affected by the blessings, too!

LEGAL REDEMPTION FROM SICKNESS AND DISEASE

You have been legally redeemed from the curse of sickness. If sickness was a part of the curse and Jesus paid the price, has the price been paid for you? Was the price enough? Did God accept it? If you are redeemed, you are bought back. You are released out of something bad into something good. You were delivered out of the realm of the curse, which included sickness, into the realm of health and blessings.

You were legally redeemed from the curse of sickness. You must take the legal provision of God's Word and demand that sickness stay away, demand that it leave your body. Faith comes when you know you've got something. When you have a legal document and someone tries to take land from you, you take the title deed to the clerk or county sheriff and say, "I've got the deed on that land. It's mine!"

Friend, you've got the title deed to health in your body. The deed is that Christ redeemed you from the curse of the law with His very own blood.

Every time someone is healed, it is a removal of the effects of the curse. Every time someone is healed, it is an administration of the effects of the blessing; one is lifted off, and the other is put on. That's the Good News we have to proclaim to people—our God reigns in all realms!

YOU OUGHT TO BE HEALED

Luke 13:10-17 gives you a graphic picture of our legal redemption.

*N*ow He was teaching in one of the synagogues on the Sabbath. And behold, there was a woman who had a spirit of infirmity eighteen years, and was bent over and could in no way raise herself up. But when Jesus saw her, He called her to Him and said to her, "Woman, you are loosed from your infirmity." And He laid His hands on her, and immediately she was made straight, and glorified God. But the ruler of the synagogue answered with indignation, because Jesus had healed on the Sabbath; and he said to the crowd, "There are six days on which men ought to work; therefore come and be healed on them, and not on the Sabbath day." The Lord then answered him and said, "Hypocrite! Does not each one of you on the Sabbath loose his ox or his donkey from the stall, and lead it away to water it? So ought not this woman, being a daughter of Abraham, whom Satan has bound—think of it— for eighteen years, be loosed from this bond on the Sabbath?" And when He said these things, all His adversaries were put to shame; and all the multitude rejoiced for all the glorious things that were done by Him.

Jesus was saying, "This woman ought to be healed, not because she has done a lot of great things, but simply because she is the daughter of Abraham."

If you have faith in Jesus Christ, then you are Abraham's seed and heirs according to the promise, too.

HEALING PROMISES

Meditate on the following promises for your healing as you speak them aloud.

I am redeemed with the blood of Jesus Christ (see 1 Pet. 1:19).

I am justified by faith, not by the works of the law (see Gal. 3:11).

I am redeemed from the curse of the law (see Gal. 3:13).

The blessings of Abraham have come upon me (see Deut. 28:1-14).

I am legally redeemed from the bondage of sickness and disease and every other work of the enemy (see Luke 13:10-17).

Chapter 5

HEALING— PROVIDED AT CALVARY

EVERYTHING that comes to us from God must come through Calvary. Every benefit of God comes to us through the completed work of Jesus in His death and resurrection.

Death entered the world through sin. "Therefore, just as through one man sin entered the world, and death through sin, and thus death spread to all men, because all sinned" (Rom. 5:12).

Before sin came, there was no sickness in the Garden. There was no sickness in Adam, but when sin entered his heart, death entered, and that process of death brought sickness and disease. When we say that sin was what brought death, and death was what eventually brought sickness upon the human race, that does not mean that a person with a handicap or a sickness has necessarily sinned.

The effects of that original sin touched the entire human race, and even today, you and I still are affected by Adam's sin. We still are battling to reclaim that which was lost in the beginning.

JESUS' MISSION

Isaiah prophesied of Jesus' work at Calvary over 700 years before Jesus' birth:

Who has believed our report? And to whom has the arm of the Lord been revealed? For He shall grow up before Him as a tender plant, and as a root out of dry ground. He has no form or comeliness; and when we see Him, there is no beauty that we should desire Him (Isaiah 53:1-2).

Jesus came forth as a green, live, viable, tender plant, someone with the life of God, but He came out of a dry ground. Israel was bone dry, a dry place, with no life.

There was nothing about Jesus' outward appearance that drew people to Him. When the tabernacle was set up in the wilderness, it was designed with beautiful royal blue, scarlet, and gold inside, candles, the golden bowl, the censer and candlesticks, and the ark of the covenant. It was beautiful inside, but the outside was covered with badger skins. It had no form or comeliness that would make you think there was anything of beauty on the inside. As the beauty of the tabernacle was on the inside so was the beauty of Christ on the inside.

"He [Jesus] is despised and rejected by men, a man of sorrows and acquainted with grief. And we hid, as it were, our faces from Him; He was despised, and we did not esteem Him" (Isa. 53:3). Jesus never was lifted up or valued as He should have been.

When Jesus showed up, they said, "Let's throw Him off a cliff" (see Luke 4:29). He was despised and rejected. He never received the honor that was due the King of kings and the Lord of lords.

Surely He has borne our griefs and carried our sorrows; yet we esteemed Him stricken, smitten by God, and afflicted (Isaiah 53:4).

The word "borne" is the Hebrew word *nasa*, which means to carry, to bear; or to take in our place. "Griefs" and "sorrows" in the Hebrew are *choli* and *makob* and mean sicknesses and pains or infirmities and diseases.

But He was wounded for our transgressions, He was bruised for our iniquities; the chastisement for our peace was upon Him, and by His stripes we are healed (Isaiah 53:5).

With His bruises, beatings, and physical punishment we are healed. We find this same thought in Matthew 8:17: "That it might be fulfilled which was spoken by Isaiah the prophet, saying: 'He Himself took our infirmities and bore our sicknesses.'"

FORGIVENESS AND HEALING
GO TOGETHER

Jesus completed a work to forgive your sins and to heal your body. Both were provided at Calvary. Scripture in First Peter 2:24 further bears out that the healing spoken of in Isaiah 53:5 was not just spiritual healing: "Who Himself bore our sins in His own body on the tree, that we, having died to sins, might live for righteousness—by whose stripes you were healed."

Jesus forgave people before the cross, and He forgave people after the cross. He said to the woman who was caught in sin, "Neither do I condemn you; go and sin no more" (John 8:11). We must remember that Jesus said, "*I am the Resurrection*" (John 11:25).

Jesus forgave sins before Calvary, He took our sins at Calvary, and He forgives sins after Calvary. It's important to establish this, because we're going to see the same thing with healing. Jesus healed the sick before Calvary, He took sickness and disease to provide healing at Calvary, and He still heals people today. Even though healing was purchased at Calvary, He healed people because He was the Healer God. Jesus was operating under the Old Covenant, which granted healing.

We see this with the healing of the woman who had the spirit of infirmity for 18 years. "So ought not this woman, being a daughter of Abraham, whom Satan has bound—think of it—for eighteen years, be loosed from this bond on the

Sabbath?" (Luke 13:16). She had a covenant right to be healed.

There are many other accounts of Jesus healing the sick before Calvary, but healing didn't stop with the end of His earthly ministry. If it did, then forgiveness for sin should also stop. Forgiveness of sin and healing are side by side in First Peter 2:24.

Jesus not only took sin from people during His three years of ministry, but at Calvary, He took the sin of the whole world in order that after Calvary all could receive forgiveness.

Jesus not only took sickness from people during the three years of His ministry, but on Calvary He bore the sickness and disease of the world in order that healing might come to all after Calvary.

Now, just because Jesus took all the sin of the world doesn't mean everyone is going to get saved. People often ask, "Well, if He took sickness and disease from everyone, why aren't more people healed?" One reason is because it isn't being taught in many places.

Faith comes by hearing. Half of the world has heard the gospel of salvation, yet millions have rejected that message, not accepting salvation. If that's true in the realm of forgiveness, then we must know it is also true in the realm of healing.

In James 5:14-15, forgiveness of sin and healing for the physical body were both provided through the prayer of faith:

Is anyone among you sick? Let him call for the elders of the church, and let them pray over him, anointing him with oil in the name of the

Lord. And the prayer of faith will save the sick, and the Lord will raise him up. And if he has committed sins, he will be forgiven.

Salvation is an all-inclusive word that has to do with the deliverance of our lives from the bondage and oppression of the enemy. It means healing, safety, preservation, wholeness, and soundness of the complete person.

James is talking about physical healing of sickness in the body and spiritual forgiveness of sin in the heart. They are distinctly separate. Both healing and forgiveness were provided at Calvary. They are redemption rights. These rights will stand in the Supreme Court of the Universe. The Man who bought and paid for both of these benefits—Jesus Himself—is seated at the right hand of the Judge.

DISCERNING THE LORD'S BODY

We are to discern the Lord's body crucified at Calvary (to acknowledge and receive all of His benefits of forgiveness, healing, and provision).

For I received from the Lord that which I also delivered to you: that the Lord Jesus on the same night in which He was betrayed took bread; and when He had given thanks, He broke it and said, "Take, eat; this is My body which is broken for you; do this in remembrance of Me." In the same manner He also took the cup after supper, saying, "This cup is the new covenant in My blood. This do, as often as you drink it, in remembrance of Me." For as often as you eat this bread and drink this cup, you proclaim the Lord's death till He comes. Therefore whoever eats this bread or drinks this cup of the Lord in an unworthy manner will be guilty of the body and blood of the Lord. But let a man examine himself, and so let him eat of that bread and drink of that cup. For he who eats and drinks in an unworthy manner eats and drinks judgment to himself, not discerning the Lord's body. For this reason many are weak and sick among you, and many sleep (1 Corinthians 11:23-30).

To discern the Lord's body also means to care for, to uplift and pray for the entire Body of Christ, of which you, as a believer, are a member. You must forgive others.

HEALING IS RELATED TO FORGIVENESS

We have a friend who has been teaching and preaching for over 60 years. Both she and her husband have ministered the fullness of the Word of God faithfully and have walked in His unfailing love and provision.

In 1964, having walked in divine health for many years, our friend was attacked by cancer. She underwent the recommended surgery, and while recuperating sought the Lord as to how or why this thing had come upon her.

God revealed to her that she had allowed unforgiveness to spring up in a root of bitterness in her heart. She had been ill treated by a sister in the church years before, and had not released the hurt and anger that followed. When her spirit bore witness to this, she knew exactly how she had allowed the devil entrance into her body. She immediately promised the Lord that as soon as she got out of the hospital she would go to that sister and resolve the difference. She did so. She totally recovered and she has not had any recurrence of cancer or any serious problem in the last 26 years!

To discern the Lord's body is to examine yourself to make sure there is nothing blocking your faith, that there is no blockage to receiving the healing Jesus bought at Calvary, understanding what Jesus did at Calvary.

HEALING PROMISES

Meditate upon the following promises as you speak them aloud.

Jesus bore my griefs (sicknesses) and carried my sorrows (pains) (see Isa. 53:4).

Jesus was wounded, bruised, and beaten for my sins, sicknesses, and diseases (see Isa. 53:5).

I am healed by the stripes of Jesus (see 1 Pet. 2:24).

I discern the Lord's body and receive all that He has provided for me, including healing for my physical body (see 1 Cor. 11:23-30).

I am diligent to pray for my brothers and sisters in Christ that they may become all God has called them to be (see 1 Cor. 11:23-30).

Love is and always
has been the
motivation behind
the healing miracles
of Jesus.

Chapter 6

HEALING— AN EXPRESSION OF GOD'S LOVE

And when Jesus went out He saw a great multitude; and He was moved with compassion for them, and healed their sick (Matthew 14:14).

JESUS was moved with compassion to heal the sick. Love is and always has been the motivation behind the healing miracles of Jesus. They were not done just to prove Jesus was God in the flesh. Although miracles are proof of Christ's divinity, miracles were performed because God loves people. He was willing to use His power to meet the needs of hurting people. His love has not changed, and He is just as willing today to heal you. He loves you as much as any other person on the face of the earth.

The love of Jesus is the same today as it was 2,000 years ago. Nothing really has changed concerning healing. God is moved by compassion to heal the sick in the 21st century just as He was in the first century.

You can be assured God's love is reaching toward you today. He is moved with compassion to heal you and make you whole.

"Love never fails [never fades out or becomes obsolete or comes to an end]..." (1 Cor. 13:8 AMP). Love will find a way when there seems to be no way. Since God is love, you can be confident that He wants you to receive His healing power.

To understand healing in the broad perspective, we should understand why Jesus came. God sent His Son because He loved people. He wants no one to perish; He offers every person eternal life.

For God so loved the world that He gave His only begotten Son, that whoever believes in Him should not perish but have everlasting life (John 3:16).

Zoe or everlasting life touches every realm of man's existence. Joy is a part of the life of God. Peace is a part of the life of God. Abundance is a part of the life of God. Fullness and fulfillment are part of the life of God. Healing, strength, power—they're all a part of God's life.

Healing is an expression of God's love for us, which says that God does not want us to perish in our bodies. He wants us to have health. God's love is to free us from perishing in our bodies.

> Sympathy feels badly for someone and identifies with their situation, while compassion moves to do something about the problem.

First John 3:8 says that Jesus came to destroy the works of the devil. Acts 10:38 carries a similar message in removing the oppression of the devil: "How God anointed Jesus of Nazareth with the Holy Spirit and with power, who went about doing good and healing all who were oppressed by the devil, for God was with Him."

Jesus came to free us from the devil's domination, which includes sickness, disease, and infirmity. He came to lift us into abundant life and health.

Jesus' compassion motive is revealed again in John 10:10 (AMP): "I came that they may have and enjoy life, and have it in abundance (to the full, till it overflows)."

Jesus' compassion is further enforced in 3 John 2 (AMP): "Beloved, I pray that you may prosper in every way and [that your body] may keep well, even as [I know] your soul keeps well and prospers."

According to God's Word, "It is appointed unto men once to die" (Heb. 9:27 KJV). Whenever a believer dies, he simply changes clothes. He gets a glorified body and goes immediately into the presence of Jesus. However, it is not the will of God that we spend our entire life with the effects of death latching on to us. It is God's will that you spend your days with the expression of life and health in your body. You are to be healthy. You are to live until you die. God's will for you is to live every day to its fullest.

Jesus healed because of compassion, and there's a big difference between sympathy and compassion. Sympathy feels badly for someone and identifies with their situation, while compassion moves to do something about the problem. Sympathy is like an automobile in "park," while compassion is in "gear." When you're in gear, you move toward someone.

The traditional view of healing is that Jesus healed sick people to prove He was the Son of God, that miracles were proof of His divinity. If miracles were done just to prove that Jesus was the Son of God, then there is no more need for miracles, because Jesus has proved that He was the divine Son of God. This theological viewpoint is the basis for many Christians rejecting healing for today.

If Jesus' reason was simply to prove who He was, that reason no longer exists, because now we have the written record of what He did. However, if Jesus healed because He was moved with compassion, then His compassion has not changed in 2,000 years. Lamentations 3:22-23 says, "His compassions fail not. They are new every morning."

Hurting people can still touch the heart of God. His compassion still flows, and when hurting people release their faith, they will receive from Him.

The miracles of Jesus affirm the fact that He was the Son of God, but that was not the reason He healed. Think of it this way. I preach on Sunday, but that's not the reason I'm the pastor of Victory Christian Center. I'm the pastor because I am called by God. Preaching is simply evidence of the calling.

Hebrews 13:8 says, "Jesus Christ is the same yesterday, today, and forever." If Jesus healed because of compassion in

His earthly ministry, then we can be assured His motivation for healing today is a heart full of compassion for all men.

HEALING PROMISES

Believe, receive, and speak the following settled legal promises regarding your healing today.

> Jesus is moved with compassion on my behalf. He wants me to be healed because of His great love for me (see Matt. 14:14).

> God wants me to have Zoe life (His kind of life) in every realm of my being (see John 10:10; 3 John 2).

> Satan cannot dominate or oppress my life because Jesus came to set me free (see 1 John 3:8; Acts 10:38).

Hurting people
can still touch the
heart of God.

Chapter 7

PAUL'S THORN IN THE FLESH

ANY people today who hear about the healing power of God refer back to Paul's thorn in the flesh and say, "Since Paul didn't get healed, why should I expect to get healed?"

Books have been written identifying Paul's "thorn" as some type of sickness, from back trouble to bad eyes! Let's see what God really said about this "thorn in the flesh."

In the following Scripture, where does it say Paul was sick?

And lest I should be exalted above measure by the abundance of the revelations, a thorn in the flesh was given to me, a messenger of Satan to buffet me, lest I be exalted above measure. Concerning this thing I pleaded with the Lord three times that it might depart from me. And He said to me, "My grace is sufficient for you, for My strength is made perfect in weakness." Therefore most gladly I will rather boast in my infirmities, that the power of Christ may rest upon me. Therefore I take pleasure in infirmities, in reproaches, in needs, in persecutions, in distresses, for Christ's sake. For when I am weak, then I am strong (2 Corinthians 12:7-10).

Where did Paul come up with the term, "thorn in the flesh"? This term is found in several other places of Scripture. We'll look at two of them.

God spoke to Moses on behalf of the children of Israel concerning the driving out of the inhabitants of the land of Canaan.

And you shall divide the land by lot as an inheritance among your families; to the larger you shall give a larger inheritance, and to the smaller you shall give a smaller inheritance; there everyone's inheritance shall be whatever falls to him by lot. You shall inherit according to the tribes of your fathers. But if you do not drive out the inhabitants of the land from before you, then it shall be that those whom you let remain shall be irritants in your eyes and thorns in your sides, and they shall harass you in the land where you dwell (Numbers 33:54-55).

When God said this, did He mean that if they didn't drive them out, these Canaanites would get in their eyes and their feet would be dangling out? Did He mean they were going to be stuck in their flesh? He meant none of these things. It was simply a figure of speech.

Have you ever heard someone say, "They are a pain in the neck"? Some of you call your neighbors, friends, and even relatives "a pain in the neck"! Well, that doesn't mean every time you see them you get a pain in your neck. It is a figure of speech. God is saying, "They will be a problem to you. They will harass you."

We see a similar figure of speech in Joshua 23:13:

*K*now *for certain that the Lord your God will no longer drive out these nations from before you. But they shall be snares and traps to you, and scourges on your sides and thorns in your eyes, until you perish from this good land which the Lord your God has given you.*

Now, the Lord is saying, "Take heed, love the Lord your God and keep His commandments, but if you don't keep the commandments and love the Lord your God, then these Canaanites will be scourges, traps, snares, and thorns in your eyes until you perish."

Have you ever heard someone say, "That's an eyesore to the community"? Now, that doesn't mean everybody gets sores in their eyes from going there. It doesn't mean some type of disease. It's a figure of speech.

A MESSENGER OF SATAN

Paul said,

And lest I should be exalted above measure by the abundance of the revelations, a thorn in the flesh was given to me, a messenger of Satan to buffet me, lest I be exalted above measure (2 Corinthians 12:7).

The word "messenger" in the Greek is *Angelos*. It is found 188 times in Scripture—181 times interpreted as *angel* and 7 times interpreted as *messenger*. Never was it used to describe a thing or sickness. It was always used to refer to a person or an angel. So when he used the word *angelos* here, he's not talking about a thing, which could be sickness or disease. He's talking about a person or a spirit being.

Who sent this spirit being of satan against Paul? Who wanted to keep Paul from being exalted into a place of authority and dominion? *Satan!* Who raised Paul up to be a great apostle? *God!* So who's trying to pull you down from your place of authority and dominion on this earth? *Satan!* Who has lifted you up to rule and reign in this life through the gift of righteousness? God!

The word "buffet" refers to continual motion, so this messenger sent from satan was continually striking at Paul everywhere he went. The "messenger" was a wicked, demonic spirit that followed Paul everywhere he traveled and stirred up the people, opposing him in everything he did. Before Paul arrived in some cities, they already wanted to stone him.

If Paul's thorn in the flesh was sickness or disease, then the greatest apostle that ever lived who wrote half the New Testament was sick all the time.

THE PERSECUTIONS OF PAUL

Paul was not sick, but he did go through intense and continual suffering and persecution. We get a better picture of the constant buffeting and persecution he received in Second Corinthians 6:4-10:

> *But in all things we commend ourselves as ministers of God: in much patience, in tribulation, in needs, in distresses, in stripes, in imprisonments, in tumults, in labors, in sleeplessness, in fastings; by purity, by knowledge, by longsuffering, by kindness, by the Holy Spirit, by sincere love, by the word of truth, by the power of God, by the armor of righteousness on the right hand and on the left, by honor and dishonor, by evil report and good report; as deceivers, and yet true; as unknown, and yet well known; as dying, and behold we live; as chastened, and yet not killed; as sorrowful, yet always rejoicing; as poor, yet making many rich; as having nothing, and yet possessing all things.*

These vicious things happened to Paul because he stood up for righteousness, he proclaimed the gospel, and he continually declared the Kingdom of God.

Jesus spoke about persecution and rejection that would come to those who become carriers of His Word.

And whoever will not receive you nor hear your words, when you depart out of that house or city, shake off the dust from your feet. Assuredly, I say to you, it will be more tolerable for the land of Sodom and Gomorrah in the day of judgment than for that city! Behold, I send you out as sheep in the midst of wolves. Therefore be wise as serpents and harmless as doves. But beware of men, for they will deliver you up to councils and scourge you in their synagogues. And you will be brought before governors and kings for My sake, as a testimony to them and to the Gentiles. But when they deliver you up, do not worry about how or what you should speak. For it will be given to you in that hour what you should speak; for it is not you who speak, but the Spirit of your Father who speaks in you. Now brother will deliver up brother to death, and a father his child; and children will rise up against parents and cause them to be put to death. And you will be hated by all men for My name's sake. But he who endures to the end will be saved. When they persecute you in this city, flee to another. For assuredly, I say to you, you will not have gone through the cities of Israel before the Son of Man comes (Matthew 10:14-23).

Jesus said there would be persecution, but did you notice in this list, there's nothing mentioned about bad eyes, sore backs, arthritis, or heart disease? Sickness is never mentioned.

The sufferings and persecutions Paul experienced are further described in Second Corinthians 11:21-33:

To our shame I say that we were too weak for that! But in whatever anyone is bold—I speak foolishly—I am bold also. Are they Hebrews? So am I. Are they Israelites? So am I. Are they the seed of Abraham? So am I. Are they ministers of Christ?—I speak as a fool—I am more: in labors more abundant, in stripes above measure, in prisons more frequently, in deaths often. From the Jews five times I received forty stripes minus one. Three times I was beaten with rods; once I was stoned; three times I was shipwrecked; a night and a day I have been in the deep; in journeys often, in perils of waters, in perils of robbers, in perils of my own countrymen, in perils of the Gentiles, in perils in the city, in perils in the wilderness, in perils in the sea, in perils among false brethren; in weariness and toil, in sleeplessness often, in hunger and thirst, in fastings often, in cold and nakedness—besides the other things, what comes upon me daily: my deep concern for all the churches. Who is weak, and I am not weak? Who is made to stumble, and I do not burn with indignation? If I must boast, I will boast in the things which concern my infirmity. The God and Father of our Lord Jesus Christ, who is blessed forever, knows that I am not lying. In Damascus the governor, under Aretas the king, was guarding the city of the Damascenes with a garrison, desiring to apprehend me; but I was let down in a basket through a window in the wall, and escaped from his hands.

When Paul listed "infirmity," he was not talking about sickness and disease. He was referring to the times he was brought to the point of total weakness because of the attack of the enemy. All four translations given on Second Corinthians 12:10 from *The New Testament From 26 Translations* (by Zondervan Publishing House, Grand Rapids, Michigan) render the word "infirmity" as weakness or humiliation.

MY GRACE IS SUFFICIENT

When Paul pleaded with the Lord for the demonic messenger to depart from him, God's response was:

My grace is sufficient for you, for My strength is made perfect in weakness (2 Corinthians 12:9).

Paul's response was:

Therefore most gladly I will rather boast in my infirmities, that the power of Christ may rest upon me. Therefore I take pleasure in infirmities, in reproaches, in needs, in persecutions, in distresses, for Christ's sake. For when I am weak, then I am strong (2 Corinthians 12:9-10).

God was saying to Paul (just as He is saying to you and me today), "When you are at your weakest point, My grace will be sufficient to meet anything the devil throws at you. When you don't have any strength, My strength will be glorified through your life."

Remember, God is not referring to sickness and disease. In another passage, Paul said, "I will rise above anything and everything the devil throws at me. Nothing can keep me down, for I am more than a conqueror in Christ Jesus." Let's look at these verses in Romans 8:35-39:

Who shall separate us from the love of Christ? Shall tribulation, or distress, or persecution, or famine, or nakedness, or peril, or sword? As it is written: "For Your sake we are killed all day long; we are accounted as sheep for the slaughter." Yet in all these things we are more than conquerors through Him who loved us. For I am persuaded that neither death nor life, nor angels nor principalities nor powers, nor things present nor things to come, nor height nor depth, nor any other created thing, shall be able to separate us from the love of God which is in Christ Jesus our Lord.

God's grace was sufficient for Paul, and it is sufficient to carry you and me through the attacks of the enemy that are hurled at us.

Paul became acquainted with the overwhelming grace of God, and he saw the magnificent power of God demonstrated again and again. He said, "I am going to take glory in my weaknesses because when I am weak, when I find myself imprisoned without cause, beaten and in stripes because of the gospel and there seems to be no way out, God, in the middle of the night, sends an earthquake and shakes the prison. Every chain is broken, every door is opened, and I walk out free! When I am in a shipwreck or I am a day and a night in the deep and have no hope, God sends His angel and says, 'All that are with you are going to be saved, Paul,' and I end up on an island preaching to everyone on the island and many get saved."

Paul is saying, "When I get to the point that I realize only God's power can change the situation, then the power of God is manifested." The Lord said, "My strength is made perfect in your weakness" (2 Cor. 12:9).

The manifestations of God's power will bring you through the buffetings of satan. God's ability will abound when your ability is weak. As long as you are self-sufficient (totally dependent upon yourself), you will not see the grace of God manifested as He wills.

If it was sickness that enabled Paul to do all the things he did, then you should pray to get the same sickness Paul supposedly had (and even more) because he did a lot of things! You must also realize, sickness today is just like it was 2,000 years ago. Sickness doesn't enable you to do more things. It limits you from doing things. Sickness sapped strength then like it saps strength today. Sickness limited people then just as it limits people today.

HANDKERCHIEFS FROM PAUL

If Paul stayed sick as some say, what kind of faith do you think sick people would have of getting an anointed handkerchief from him?

*N*ow God worked unusual miracles by the hands of Paul, so that even handkerchiefs or aprons were brought from his body to the sick, and the disease left them and the evil spirits went out of them (Acts 19:11-12).

I hope you realize how utterly ridiculous and illogical the idea is that Paul was sick all the time. Paul laid hands on sick people so they would be well. Some declare Paul had a bad back. You don't inspire people to faith when you are limping because of back pain or when you have pus running out of your eyes! If these things were true, can you imagine Paul saying, "Come, let me pray for you. I want to lay hands on you so you can become just like me"?

None of these accounts of Paul's buffetings and afflictions talk about sickness, but they all talk of the persecution and buffetings of the devil that came against him to stop him from preaching the gospel.

When Paul sought the Lord to remove the messenger of satan, God said, "Paul, I am going to demonstrate the victory of My resurrection power through your life. You will defeat the devil in everything you do, no matter what he throws against your life. My glory and power will rest upon you, and you are going to demonstrate before the whole world the defeat of satan."

Friend, God is no respecter of persons. He is speaking this same message to you today! So I would simply say to you, "Arise [from the depression and prostration in which circumstances have kept you—rise to a new life]! Shine (be radiant with the glory of the Lord), for your light has come, and the glory of the Lord has risen upon you!" (Isa. 60:1 AMP).

HEALING PROMISES

Let's again review some of the healing promises provided at Calvary for you, which have been covered in this chapter. Meditate upon these promises as you read them aloud.

> Just as God's grace was sufficient to cause Paul to overcome all of satan's buffetings, God's grace causes me to overcome satan's buffetings. Christ Jesus causes me to triumph in every area of life (see 2 Cor. 12:9-10).

> I will rise above anything and everything the devil throws at me. Nothing can keep me down, for I am more than a conqueror in Christ Jesus (see Rom. 8:35-39).

> Today I will rise to new life from the depression and prostration in which circumstances have kept me (see Isa. 60:1).

Chapter 8

HOW TO
LIVE LONGER

*T**he days of our lives are seventy years; and if
by reason of strength they are eighty years...*
(Psalm 90:10).

Ephesians 6:1-3 indicates that your days upon the earth
can be determined by how you treat your parents:

*C**hildren, obey your parents in the Lord, for
this is right. "Honor your father and mother," which is the first commandment with promise: "That it may be well with you and you may live
long on the earth."*

This is the first commandment God gave that had a promise with it. The condition: "Obey your parents in the Lord."

The promise: "It may be well with you and you may live long on the earth."

Exodus 20:12 says it this way: "Honor your father and your mother, that your days may be long upon the land which the Lord your God is giving you."

Psalm 91:14-16 promises long life if you set your love upon God and make Him your refuge:

Because he has set his love upon Me, therefore I will deliver him; I will set him on high, because he has known My name. He shall call upon Me, and I will answer him; I will be with him in trouble; I will deliver him and honor him. With long life I will satisfy him, and show him My salvation.

Living a long life doesn't just happen because you hear a promise from God's Word. You must use wisdom, knowledge, and understanding

Proverbs 3:13 says, "Happy is the man who finds wisdom, and the man who gains understanding."

I believe the Lord gave me a word of knowledge concerning flying airplanes! Since we were traveling many places in ministry, I had gotten my private license and instrument rating for flying. I am convinced it was the grace of God that kept us during those times, because most people who fly, love to fly. I, on the other hand, didn't care a thing about flying an airplane. I did it because it was a quick, efficient means of transportation, freeing us to go more places. The trouble was, I'd jump in the plane and take off without really concentrating on what I was doing. I would be thinking about the next service or other upcoming events, not realizing the dangerous situation I was creating.

Finally, the Spirit of God got through to me that I should not be flying small planes. The day came when I decided to believe God for the money to pay the airlines to take us where we needed to go! Now, all this may not seem like any great revelation to you, but it was to me. There are natural as well as spiritual things we can do to live longer.

For her proceeds (of wisdom and understanding) are better than the profits of silver, and her gain than fine gold. She is more precious than rubies, and all the things you may desire cannot compare with her. Length of days is in her right hand, and in her left hand riches and honor (Proverbs 3:14-16).

Proverbs 9:9-11 says the days of the person operating in wisdom and understanding will be multiplied and his years will be increased:

Give instruction to a wise man, and he will be still wiser; teach a just man, and he will increase in learning. The fear of the Lord is the beginning of wisdom, and the knowledge of the Holy One is understanding. **For by me thy days will be multiplied, and years of life will be added to you.**

Proverbs 10:27 says, "The *fear of the Lord* prolongs days, but the years of the wicked will be shortened." "Fear of the Lord" means obedience to the Lord. It pays to be obedient! Long life is one of its benefits! If you go beyond God's grace for a time or season in your life, you are in danger. Obey God. Stop when He says to stop and start when He says to start.

NOAH'S LIFE EXTENDED

Noah extended his life and the lives of his family members through obedience to the Lord, even when he was mocked by the men and women of the world as he began building an ark in a dry season. Noah, however, had revelation from the Lord as to what was going to happen. He prepared the ark to avoid the calamity and destruction that would result when the flood came.

MOSES AND THE ISRAELITES DELIVERED

Moses and the Israelites were delivered from the Red Sea in front of them and Pharaoh's army behind them when Moses obeyed the word of the Lord.

> "...Stretch out your hand over the sea, that the waters may come back upon the Egyptians, on their chariots, and on their horsemen." And Moses stretched out his hand over the sea; and when the morning appeared, the sea returned to its full depth, while the Egyptians were fleeing into it. So the Lord overthrew the Egyptians in

the midst of the sea. Then the waters returned and covered the chariots, the horsemen, and all the army of Pharaoh that came into the sea after them. Not so much as one of them remained. But the children of Israel had walked on dry land in the midst of the sea, and the waters were a wall to them on their right hand and on their left. So the Lord saved Israel that day out of the hand of the Egyptians, and Israel saw the Egyptians dead on the seashore. Thus Israel saw the great work which the Lord had done in Egypt; so the people feared the Lord, and believed the Lord and His servant Moses (Exodus 14:26-31).

LONGER LIFE FOR DANIEL AND THE THREE HEBREW CHILDREN

How about old Daniel when he spent an evening in the lions' den? The angel of the Lord showed up and shut the lions' mouths. Remember, the king himself fasted that night for Daniel. He didn't want to throw Daniel in the den, but he wouldn't back off of the word he had given.

Then Daniel said to the king, "O king, live forever! My God sent His angel and shut the lions' mouths, so that they have not hurt me, because I was found innocent before Him; and also, O king, I have done no wrong before you." Then the king was exceedingly glad for him, and commanded that they should take Daniel up out

of the den. So Daniel was taken up out of the den,
and no injury whatever was found on him, because
he believed in his God (Daniel 6:21-23).

The lives of three Hebrew boys—Shadrach, Meshach, and Abednego—were delivered by the confession of their lips. They proclaimed that their God was able to deliver them, which He did.

*S*hadrach, *Meshach, and Abednego answered*
and said to the king, "O Nebuchadnezzar,
we have no need to answer you in this matter.
If that is the case, our God whom we serve is
able to deliver us from the burning fiery fur-
nace, and He will deliver us from your hand, O
king. But if not, let it be known to you, O king,
that we do not serve your gods, nor will we
worship the gold image which you have set up"
(Daniel 3:16-18).

PETER'S LIFE EXTENDED

Peter's life was spared, even though he had been imprisoned and was scheduled for execution. Because of the constant prayer offered for him by the church, an angel of the Lord came to him in the prison and brought supernatural deliverance to him.

*P*eter *was therefore kept in prison, but con-*
stant prayer was offered for him by the

> The healthier you are, the more you can do for the Kingdom of God.

church. *And when Herod was about to bring him out, that night Peter was sleeping, bound with two chains between two soldiers; and the guards before the door were keeping the prison. Now behold, an angel of the Lord stood by him, and a light shone in the prison; and he struck Peter on the side and raised him up, saying, "Arise quickly!" And his chains fell off his hands. Then the angel said to him, "Gird yourself and tie on your sandals"; and so he did. And he said to him, "Put on your garment and follow me." So he went out and followed him, and did not know that what was done by the angel was real, but thought he was seeing a vision. When they were past the first and the second guard posts, they came to the iron gate that leads to the city, which opened to them of its own accord; and they went out and went down one street, and immediately the angel departed from him* (Acts 12:5-10).

The days of supernatural deliverance are not over. God will do whatever is needed to protect and deliver His own!

PAUL'S LIFE SPARED

Paul and the lives of the people on board a ship were spared when they were shipwrecked at Malta. Paul received a visitation from an angel of the Lord who said all the lives would be spared, but the ship would be destroyed.

> *For there stood by me this night an angel of the God to whom I belong and whom I serve, saying, "Do not be afraid, Paul; you must be brought before Caesar; and indeed God has granted you all those who sail with you." Therefore take heart, men, for I believe God that it will be just as it was told me (Acts 27:23-25).*

LONG LIFE IS GOD'S PLAN FOR YOU

Longer life, obviously, is the outcome when you walk hand in hand with the Lord on a daily basis, when you are obedient to His voice and sensitive to the leadings of the Holy Spirit, for then God will move all Heaven if need be just to protect and preserve your life! Hallelujah!

God wants you to have long life, for you are needed in the earth more than you are needed in Heaven. When someone has gone to be with the Lord prematurely, often people say, "God needed them more in Heaven."

If there ever was a need for someone full of the power of the Holy Ghost, full of faith, and full of the message of the gospel of the Lord Jesus Christ, the need is here on the earth now.

If God needed all of the Christians in Heaven, He would take you home the moment you were born again. God has a better plan than just getting you saved and rushing you into Heaven! He wants to use you. He needs you here in the earth to spread the fragrance of the knowledge of Him throughout the world. That's the reason that the healthier you are, the more you can do for the Kingdom of God.

HEALING PROMISES

Long life is yours as you obey the Word of the Lord. Believe, speak, meditate, and receive the scriptural promises in this chapter.

The days of my life are 70 years...80 if by reason of strength (see Ps. 90:10).

Long life is mine because I obey and honor my parents in the Lord (see Eph. 6:1-3; Exod. 20:12).

Long life is mine because I set my love upon the Lord (see Ps. 91:14-16).

My application of godly wisdom and understanding assures me of long life (see Prov. 3:13-16; 9:9-11).

My obedience to the Lord prolongs my life (see Prov. 10:27).

God's supernatural protection and provision are mine, just as it was manifested to the patriarchs of old (see Exod. 14; Dan. 3,6; Acts 12; Acts 27).

Chapter 9

YOUR APPOINTMENT WITH DEATH

Q UESTIONS about death always come when divine healing is presented. How does a person die if he doesn't get sick? Death can come by a person's simply releasing his spirit to God. The medical records would indicate the heart stopped working, which is the natural effect of the spirit departing from a human being.

Paul knew when his time of departure had come. He had a choice to leave or to remain.

A ccording to my earnest expectation and hope that in nothing I shall be ashamed, but that with all boldness, as always, so now also Christ will be magnified in my body, whether by life or by death. For to me, to live is Christ, and to die is gain. But if I live on in the flesh, this will mean fruit from my labor; yet what I shall choose I cannot tell. For I am hard pressed between the two, having a desire to depart and be with Christ, which is far better. Nevertheless to remain in the flesh is more needful for you. And being confident of this, I know that I shall remain and continue with you all for your progress and joy of faith, that your rejoicing for me may be more abundant in Jesus Christ by my coming to you again (Philippians 1:20-26).

When it came time for Paul to die, he knew it and said, "I'm ready to go." But he realized he had something deposited in him by the revelation he had received of Jesus Christ and that if he could get that into people, their whole lives would be enriched, their faith would be increased, they could abound and walk in God in a greater dimension.

Imagine that! A man deciding whether he's going to die or live! I say to you, "The decision is yours." It has been proven medically time and time again that the will to live can cause people with terminal illnesses to live for many years. Some are even totally healed, while others who lose the will to live die untimely deaths of diseases that should not have killed them. When you hook your faith and your will up with the will of God, you can live a long, fulfilling life.

Paul had finished his course. But he made the decision to remain longer to be a blessing to the people. If he had a choice to remain longer, then you also have a choice if you are "in Christ."

Paul said:

For I am already being poured out as a drink offering, and the time of my departure is at hand. I have fought the good fight, I have finished the race, I have kept the faith. Finally, there is laid up for me the crown of righteousness, which the Lord, the righteous Judge, will give to me on that Day, and not to me only but also to all who have loved His appearing (2 Timothy 4:6-8).

When you go to the airport, there's a specific time of departure for your flight. Similarly, it was as if Paul was looking at the clock and he said, "The time of my departure is at hand." Hebrews 9:27 (KJV) says, "It is appointed unto men once to die." Now, here's how I am encouraging you to die when your appointed time comes.

Psalm 104:29 (AMP) says, "When You hide Your face, they are troubled and dismayed; when You take away their breath, they die and return to their dust."

God takes away the breath, and the word here for breath is *Ruwach* or in the English translation, *Ruach*. *Ruach* means "spirit." Remember in Genesis where God breathed into man the "breath" of life? He breathed "spirit" into Adam's body.

If you die by the Lord's taking away your breath, then what would be the medical explanation? Heart failure. In other words, if you quit breathing, your heart will stop. They may discover in an examination that there was no heart attack. The heart just quit beating. In other words, the body functions just stop.

Smith Wigglesworth died this way. He told the people around him he was going home. It appears this is the way Abraham died. He told everyone good-bye and took off!

Wouldn't you rather see a loved one die this way than die through torment and suffering? It all begins with believing that it's God's will that we be in health.

I've had people say to me, "Well, if you believe in divine healing, then that means you believe people will never die." No, because the Bible says it is appointed unto men once to die. There is an appointment with death for each person who is not raptured. Just don't leave too soon because of sickness.

In Matthew 9:29, Jesus said, "According to your faith let it be to you." If it's according to your faith concerning the healing of your body, then it could be according to your faith concerning your home-going.

> There is an appointment with death for each person who is not raptured. Just don't leave too soon because of sickness.

Your time for home-going, like Paul's, should come only after you have "fought a good fight...finished [your] course...kept the faith" (2 Tim. 4:7 KJV).

HEALING PROMISES

Divine health is yours until the moment of your "appointed time" to go home to be with the Lord.

Make these confessions aloud, believing that God wants your "long life" to end with a peaceful home-going.

Like Paul, I will go home once I've completed the course God has set for my life (see Phil. 1:20-26; 2 Tim. 4:6-8; Heb. 9:27).

When it is time for me to go home to be with the Lord, I will just let go and take off (see Ps. 104:29; Matt. 9:29)!

Unbelief dishonors God.
It denies God.
It is a rejection of
who God is, and it keeps
a person from receiving.

Chapter 10

HINDRANCES TO HEALING

SOME of the most common reasons why people fail to receive their healing are:

1. Unbelief can be one of the blockages to not receiving your healing. Remember what happened to Jesus Himself in His own hometown? "And He did not do many works of power there, because of their unbelief (their lack of faith in the divine mission of Jesus)" (Matt. 13:58 AMP).

Unbelief dishonors God. It denies God. It is a rejection of who God is, and it keeps a person from receiving.

2. Lack of knowledge can keep you from receiving from God, whether it be in the area of healing, finances, or anything else. Hosea 4:6 says, "My people are destroyed for lack of knowledge." Your faith cannot go beyond your knowledge. You can hope, desire, wish, or long for something beyond your knowledge, but you can only have faith in something you know. Once you know it is God's will to heal you, you are free to reach out and receive it.

3. Wavering will keep you from receiving your healing. You cannot have faith for the power of God to work in your life if you are double-minded. James made that very clear.

> *But if any of you lacks wisdom, let him ask of God, who gives to all men generously and without reproach, and it will be given to him. But let him ask in faith without any doubting, for the one who doubts is like the surf of the sea driven and tossed by the wind. For let not that man expect that he will receive anything from the Lord, being a double-minded man, unstable in all his ways* (James 1:5-8 NASB).

Once it is settled in your heart that it is God's will to heal you, you can know when you ask of God that your prayers are heard and answered. You're no longer wishing. You're not saying, "Well, you know, I'm hoping and praying. I pitched a prayer up there last week, and I hope He catches it."

First John 6:14-15 says:

> *Now this is the confidence that we have in Him, that if we ask anything according to His will, He hears us. And if we know that He hears us, whatever we ask, we know that we have the petitions that we have asked of Him.*

> Your level of faith is determined by the level of the knowledge of the Word of God inside you, because faith comes by hearing the Word.

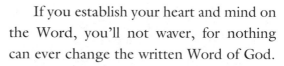

If you establish your heart and mind on the Word, you'll not waver, for nothing can ever change the written Word of God.

4. Failure to recognize the author of sickness and disease can be another reason why healing doesn't manifest. Acts 10:38 identifies satan as the author of oppression. (Sickness and disease certainly fall into the category of "oppression.") John 10:10 identifies satan as the one who steals, kills, and destroys. Sickness and disease come to steal, kill, and destroy. They come from the devil.

You'd be amazed how many people are wrestling over this one, saying, "God gave me this sickness, this disease, this infirmity, this problem in order to shape me to be the diamond He wants me to be." No way! Remember, God shapes through His Word—not through the works of satan.

Hebrews 4:12 (AMP) says:

For the Word that God speaks is alive and full of power [making it active, operative, energizing and effective]; it is sharper than any two-edged sword, penetrating to the dividing line of the breath of life (soul) and [the immortal] spirit, and of joints and marrow [of the deepest parts of our nature], exposing and sifting and analyzing and judging the very thoughts and purposes of the heart.

Establish your heart in the fact that "God is a good God, and the devil is a bad devil."

5. Another reason why many people aren't healed is they don't have the seed of the Word settled in their hearts. For example, you often hear people say, "I prayed, believed, and nothing happened."

A farmer can go on an unplowed, unplanted field and pray until he is blue in the face. He can believe all he wants to, but there will be no crop on that field until it is plowed up and the seed is sown, fertilized, watered, and protected until it comes to maturity.

This is the issue with a lot of people on healing. They want to harvest a crop of healing when they haven't sown the right seed in their heart.

When a farmer plants a seed in the ground, he leaves it there. He knows it is working, because he put it there. It's the same principle with the planting of the seed (the Word) of healing in your heart. Your heart is the soil, the Word of God is the seed, and it will produce 30-, 60-, or 100-fold if the soil is good and if you get past the devil's tactics to steal it. Tribulation, persecution, and affliction will come to try to steal the Word out of your heart. Thorns will come, which are the lust of riches and other things and the cares of this life.

Once seed has been planted in the heart, many people dig it up with their own words of doubt, wavering, and unbelief.

So how do you keep the seed of the Word of God in your heart? Meditation of the Word will cause it to germinate in your heart and then spring forth into an abundant crop of healing. Meditation of the Word means to chew on the Word or to mutter it over and over and over to yourself. Here's an example of what chewing on the Word looks like:

My God is working mightily in me. He is doing exceedingly abundantly above all I ask or think. The truth sets me free. Greater is He who is in me than he who is in the world. By Jesus' stripes I am healed.

What begins to happen as you meditate the Word? Scripture says the Word will work *effectually* in those who believe. Working "effectually" means that it will work and have an effect. It will produce power. The Word is life to you, and it is health to all your flesh.

The Word is a live dynamo working inside of you, producing the power of resurrection day and night. Your spirit man has the capacity to reproduce the very life of God in your mortal body. You are walking with the life of God flowing through you and out of you to others.

Proverbs 4:23 says, "Keep [guard] your heart with all diligence, for out of it spring the issues of life." Guard your heart, for it is out of your heart (your spirit) that healing will be released into your body.

Your level of faith is determined by the level of the knowledge of the Word of God inside you, because faith comes by hearing the Word. It's not a matter of a person's not being able to believe.

It's possible to have great faith for the forgiveness of your sins, great faith for loving someone who is unlovely, great faith to endure great struggles, yet no faith concerning healing. The same is true in the area of finances or in any other area.

Perhaps you've never heard of praying for money or believing God to return a financial seed you have planted. You begin to find out what God says and suddenly you begin to have faith for finances. Yet, you had faith all the time for many other things in your life. You had faith that Jesus died on the cross, faith that He was raised, faith that your sins were forgiven, but you can't release faith in other areas until the knowledge of the Word comes. Healing will be produced in your life on the basis of the Word you have placed in your heart.

6. Another reason people aren't healed is they don't "see" themselves whole through the eye of faith. See yourself whole. See your body out of the wheelchair and off of that bed of affliction. See your mind sound. See your limbs straightened. See your bodily organs functioning according to the perfection in which God created them. See the result of God's healing power working in your life. See the Word working in your life. See your body totally void of sickness and disease. See it as clearly as you see your own hand in front of your face! Let it become real to you, because God's Word is eternal. Second Corinthians 5:7 says, "For we walk by faith, not by sight."

> God made your body to work in perfect, divine harmony, so that out of your spirit man would flow rivers of living water—joy, peace, love, kindness, longsuffering, gentleness, goodness, mercy, faithfulness

OPEN DOORS TO SICKNESS AND DISEASE

Sin and rebellion can open the door to sickness and disease in your life. Why did sickness and disease come on the Egyptians? Did God just look down from Heaven and say, "You know, I don't like Egyptians. There's something about those fellows down there that just ticks me off"? Can you imagine what would have happened to the Egyptians if they had blessed the children of Israel? The favor of God would have come on their land, but they continually hardened their hearts. There's a law of sowing and reaping. Sickness and disease have a way of entrance through sin and rebellion. Satan began in rebellion against God.

Cancer is a form of rebellion. It is a revolt of cells inside a certain part of the body that act in rebellion against the rest of the cells—a group of "outlaw" cells try to multiply and take over. If the person with cancer will start ministering faith to his body, he can put down the rebellion in his body through the law of the Spirit of life in Christ Jesus. Cancer can be stopped by the power of faith. When someone is prayed for and they are healed of cancer through prayer, the rebellion is put down.

Sickness and disease are not normal to the body. The body was made for health. Sickness and disease are an invasion and an intrusion. They are a discrepancy in the pattern and plan God made for the body. God made your body to work in perfect, divine harmony, so that out of your spirit man would flow rivers of living water—joy, peace, love, kindness, longsuffering, gentleness, goodness, mercy, faithfulness—all those fruits would flow up out of you. He made your mind in such a way that you would think things that are good and true, just, pure, lovely, and of good report. God made your body in such a way that it would respond with health to the reactions that are taking place in your spirit and in your soul.

Proverbs 17:22 says, "A merry heart does good, like medicine, but a broken spirit dries the bones."

The Word says, "The joy of the Lord is your strength" (Neh. 8:10). Joy, a positive force in your spirit, can produce strength in your physical body. What happens in your spirit can affect your physical body.

Have you ever noticed when someone speaks an ugly word to you or you receive a disappointment, sometimes you will have a physical attack that comes alongside it? It has been proven that the immune system is at its lowest place of defense when the body or the mind is under intense stress over prolonged periods.

Strife, bitterness, and unforgiveness can be open doors to sickness and disease. God is the Master Designer, and He created you to work in such perfect synchronization that your spirit, soul, and body would all work together for your wholeness. When you rejoice and have peace in your heart, it causes the glands in your body to work as they were designed to function. On the other hand, the opposite takes place when strife or bitterness enters your heart.

Someone who has anger or guilt may say, "My stomach is all tied up in knots." They're not just kidding! Their gland system is tied up. There are things in their body that won't function like they're supposed to function. Chemical substances aren't released as they should be, and others are released in wrong proportions.

> Joy, a positive force in your spirit, can produce strength in your physical body.

Daily meditate on these verses of Scripture, and God will cleanse your heart of strife and bitterness.

Let no foul or polluting language, nor evil word nor unwholesome or worthless talk [ever] come out of your mouth, but only such [speech] as is good and beneficial to the spiritual progress of others, as is fitting to the need and the occasion, that it may be a blessing and give grace (God's favor) to those who hear it. And do not grieve the Holy Spirit of God, [do not offend or vex or sadden Him] by Whom you were sealed (marked, branded as God's own, secured) for the day of redemption (of final deliverance through Christ from evil and the consequences of sin). Let all bitterness and indignation and wrath (passion, rage, bad temper) and resentment (anger, animosity) and quarreling (brawling, clamor, contention) and slander (evil-speaking, abusive or blasphemous language) be banished from you, with all malice (spite, ill will, or baseness of any kind). And become useful and helpful and kind to one another, tenderhearted (compassionate, understanding, loving-hearted), forgiving one another [readily and freely], as God in Christ forgave you (Ephesians 4:29-32 AMP).

If unforgiveness has been a problem, daily meditate on the following verses of Scripture. Make a decision to line your will up with God's Word, which is His will. Loose God's love and faith over those who have wronged you. As you set them free, you, too, will be free.

*L*ove endures long and is patient and kind; love never is envious nor boils over with jealousy; is not boastful or vainglorious, does not display itself haughtily. It is not conceited (arrogant and inflated with pride); it is not rude (unmannerly) and does not act unbecomingly. Love (God's love in us) does not insist on its own rights or its own way, for it is not self-seeking; it is not touchy or fretful or resentful; it takes no account of the evil done to it [it pays no attention to a suffered wrong]. It does not rejoice at injustice and unrighteousness, but rejoices when right and truth prevail. Love bears up under anything and everything that comes, is ever ready to believe the best of every person, its hopes are fadeless under all circumstances, and it endures everything [without weakening]. Love never fails [never fades out or becomes obsolete or comes to an end] (1 Corinthians 13:4-8 AMP).

> Strife, bitterness, and unforgiveness can be open doors to sickness and disease.

If you will walk in the pathway of life and righteousness and do what God's Word says, you will walk with a sound mind, with a spirit overflowing with *Zoe* (the God-kind of life), and with your body abounding in health.

Perhaps you are saying, "Nobody can live that way all the time." This is where God's grace and mercy come in. Simply pray, "Lord, by Your grace, forgive me." Then, start over and receive God's mercy for your failures. You may not be there now, but things can change for the better.

IS HEALING FOR EVERYONE?

Healing is for everyone, just as salvation is for everyone. Just as not everyone accepts Jesus Christ as Lord and Savior, likewise, not everyone accepts the message of healing. The rejection is on the part of the person, not on the part of God, for it is His will that every person in the earth receive His blessings.

Though God's benefits are for all, they specifically come to those who enter into covenant with Him, to those who believe what is in His covenant, to those who are in league with Him, and to those who persevere to obtain what God has promised.

You see, God will be true, though every man is a liar. God's promises—all of them—are "Yes" and "Amen." They do not change. If no one in the whole world but you gets saved, you should stand upon God's Word, believe it, and go to Heaven. You do not base your faith for salvation on whether someone else fails to respond to the gospel. You base your faith for salvation on His Word.

One of the biggest problems in the area of healing is that people often take their eyes off of the Word of God and off of Jesus and place them on the experiences of others. They look at other people and say, "Well, if that person didn't get healed, then who am I to get healed?"

Even if others prayed and it didn't happen to them, don't let that change your stand. You need to be healed. You believe God and what He said in His Word and go for the "best" He has in spite of anything that happens around you. His "best" is healing and wholeness in every realm of your life.

Healing is for everyone, just as salvation is for everyone.

Chapter 11

STATE YOUR CASE

*P*ut Me in remembrance; let us contend
together; state your case, that you may be
acquitted (Isaiah 43:26).

I*F* you are waiting for the full manifestation of healing to
come into your body or mind, put God in remembrance
of His Word.

The widow woman moved the heart of the unjust judge
because she continually presented her case to him. She persist-
ed in presenting her case to him until he gave in and ruled
favorably in her behalf.

*T*hen He spoke a parable to them, that men
always ought to pray and not lose heart, saying, "There was in a certain city a judge who did
not fear God nor regard man. Now there was a
widow in that city; and she came to him, saying,

'Avenge me of my adversary.' And he would not for a while; but afterward he said within himself, 'Though I do not fear God nor regard man, yet because this widow troubles me I will avenge her, lest by her continual coming she weary me.'" Then the Lord said, *"Hear what the unjust judge said. And shall God not avenge His own elect who cry out day and night to Him, though He bears long with them? I tell you that He will avenge them speedily..."* (Luke 18:1-8).

Put God in remembrance of your situation by speaking His Word. Jesus defeated satan by "It is written." You can defeat him in this way, too.

Let's review the "Healing Promises" that are legally yours by inheritance as a heir of God and a joint-heir of Jesus Christ. Meditate upon these promises daily. Speak them aloud, putting God in remembrance of His promises.

By Jesus' stripes I am healed
(see 1 Pet. 2:24).

It is God's will that I prosper and be in health,
just as my soul prospers
(see 3 John 2).

The Lord is my healer
(see Exod. 15:26).

Jesus came that I may enjoy life and have
it in overflowing abundance
(see John 10:10).

As I serve the Lord,
sickness is taken from my midst
(see Exod. 23:25).

Healing is one of God's benefits for me
(see Ps. 103:3).

Jesus is the serpent on the pole lifted up in the
New Covenant for my healing and deliverance
(see John 3:14).

God sent His Word and healed me
(see Ps. 107:20).

I pay attention to God's Word,
for it is life and health to me
(see Prov. 4:20-22).

God gives me good and perfect gifts.
He has no sickness or disease to give me
(see James 1:17).

As I submit to God and resist the devil,
he must flee from me.
Sickness and disease must flee from me
(see James 4:7).

Jesus is able and willing to heal me
(see Matt. 8:1-2).

Jesus can heal me through my believing,
receiving, and speaking His Word or through
the touch of another believer who is
empowered by the Holy Ghost
(see Mark 16:18).

Jesus already paid for all sin
and sickness at Calvary
(see Matt. 8:17).

Jesus is the same yesterday, today, and forever
(see Heb. 13:8)

Because the Lord is my refuge and habitation,
no evil or plague shall come nigh my dwelling
(see Ps. 91:9-11).

I am redeemed with the blood of Jesus Christ
(see 1 Pet. 1:19).

I am justified by faith, not by works of the law
(see Gal. 3:11).

Jesus redeemed me from the curse of the law
(see Gal. 3:13).

The blessings of Abraham have come upon me
(see Deut. 28:1-14).

Jesus legally redeemed me from
the bondage of sickness and disease and
every other work of the enemy
(see Luke 13:10-17).

Jesus bore my griefs (sicknesses)
and carried my sorrows (pains)
(see Isa. 53:4).

Jesus was wounded, bruised, and beaten
for my sins, sicknesses, and diseases
(see Isa. 53:5).

I am healed by the stripes of Jesus
(see 1 Pet. 2:24).

I discern the Lord's body and receive all that
He has provided for me, including healing
for my physical body
(see 1 Cor. 11:23-30).

I am diligent to pray for my brothers and sisters
in Christ that they may become all
God has called them to be
(see 1 Cor. 11:23-30).

To touch Jesus is to be made whole.
I touch Jesus today through prayer and faith
(see Mark 5:25-34).

The resurrection power of Jesus Christ flows
from my tongue as I speak words of life
(see Prov. 18:21).

I have been given authority in the name of Jesus to
speak to the mountains that I face. As I command
the mountains of sickness, despair, hopelessness, and
lack to be removed in Jesus' name, they must go and
be replaced with the fullness of God's blessings
(see Mark 11:22-23).

Because I meditate on the Word of God day and
night, God's prosperity and success are
overtaking me in all realms of life
(see Josh. 1:8).

I devour God's Word as a daily diet, for His

Word is life and health to my flesh

(see Prov. 4:20-22).

The measure of faith God gave me is

growing by leaps and bounds

(see Rom. 12:3).

Because my faith is growing,

nothing is impossible unto me

(see Matt. 17:20).

Jesus is moved with compassion on my behalf.

He wants me to be healed because

of His great love for me

(see Matt. 14:14).

God wants me to have Zoe life

(His kind of life) in every realm of my being

(see John 10:10; 3 John 2).

Satan cannot dominate or oppress my life
because Jesus came to set me free
(see 1 John 3:8; Acts 10:38).

Just as God's grace was sufficient to cause Paul to
overcome all of satan's buffetings, God's grace
causes me to overcome satan's buffetings. Christ
Jesus causes me to triumph in every area of life
(see 2 Cor. 12:9-10).

I will rise above anything and everything the
devil throws at me. Nothing can keep me down,
for I am more than a conqueror in Christ Jesus
(see Rom. 8:35-39).

Today I will rise to new life from
the depression and prostration in which
circumstances have kept me
(see Isa. 60:1).

Jesus is the author of abundant life,
while it is satan who steals, kills, and destroys
(see John 10:10).

The days of my life are 70 years…
and if by reason of strength 80
(see Ps. 90:10).

Long life is mine because I obey and
honor my parents in the Lord
(see Eph. 6:1-3; Exod. 20:12).

Long life is mine because
I set my love upon the Lord
(see Ps. 91:14-16).

My application of godly wisdom and
understanding brings long life
(see Prov. 3:13-16; 9:9-11).

My obedience to the Lord prolongs my life
(see Prov. 10:27).

God's supernatural protection and provision
are mine, just as it was manifested to
the patriarchs of old
(see Exod. 14; Dan. 3,6; Acts 12,27).

ABOUT THE AUTHOR

BILLY JOE DAUGHERTY, pastor of Victory Christian Center in Tulsa, Oklahoma, is a soul-winner with a world vision. He is founder of Victory Christian School, Victory Bible Institute, and Victory World Missions Training Center with the goals of training students to be effective Christians worldwide. Believing that "the greatest tool of evangelism in the coming days will be the local church," Billy Joe emphasizes the ministry of the individual believer in the many outreaches of Victory Christian Center.

Graduates of Oral Roberts University, Billy Joe and his wife, Sharon, have traveled extensively around the country ministering the Word of God and the love of God.

Billy Joe's daily radio and television programs bring encouragement and sound teaching into many homes.

TO CONTACT THE AUTHOR, WRITE:

Billy Joe Daugherty
Victory Christian Center
7700 South Lewis Avenue
Tulsa, OK 74136-7700

Please include your prayer requests
and comments when you write.